THE ROMAN ARMY

An Illustrated Study

by

GRAHAM WEBSTER, M.A., PH.D., F.S.A., A.M.A.
formerly Curator, Grosvenor Museum, Chester.

Reader in Romano-British Archaeology,
Department of Extra-Mural Studies,
The University of Birmingham.

PUBLICATION OF THE GROSVENOR MUSEUM, CHESTER
REVISED EDITION 1973

Printed in England by
C. Tinling & Co., Ltd., London & Prescot.

FOREWORD

THE author wishes to thank Professors I. A. Richmond and E. Birley of Durham University for considerable help received in compiling this booklet; Mr. Noel Jones for Greek and Latin translations; and Mr. F. H. Thompson, his successor as Curator of the Grosvenor Museum, for seeing the booklet through the press.

Thanks are due also to the Trustees of the British Museum for the loan of the block of the legionary helmet and for permitting the publication of this and the sword and scabbard; to the University of Wales Press for the block of the Chester fortress; to the Museums Association for the block of the Corbridge scale armour; and to the Lincoln Archaeological Research Committee for the loan of the block of the reconstruction of the legionary defences at Lincoln.

GRAHAM WEBSTER

FOREWORD TO REVISED EDITION

IT IS now seventeen years since this little booklet appeared. It has proved to be extremely popular but has now become out of date with the advance of knowledge, particularly with the excavations in Chester itself. I have endeavoured to incorporate the results of new discoveries and new thinking about the Army and I have brought the bibliography at the end up-to-date.

I am most grateful to the present Curator of the Grosvenor Museum, Mr. Dennis Petch, for allowing me to make these revisions and for his constant kindness and help in bringing new information about Chester to my attention. He has also replaced my original plan of the fortress with a more-up-to-date one of his own, for which I am also grateful.

I would like to acknowledge the help received from the Curator and his staff in preparing the revised text for publication, and seeing it through the press.

GRAHAM WEBSTER

THE ROMAN ARMY—AN INTRODUCTION

DURING the first two centuries of the Empire the Roman Army was composed of the following elements :

1. *The Praetorian Guards* or Imperial bodyguards, which the Emperor took with him on campaigns, were responsible for protecting his person and were normally stationed in Rome. Their deep personal loyalty to the Emperor made this force an important political factor.

2. *The Legions* were the main first-line troops, all Roman citizens ; there were at different times between 25 and 35 legions, almost all stationed in the frontier provinces.

3. *The Auxilia*, as their name implies, were originally a force of native allies led by their own chiefs, assisting the Roman citizen army. When Augustus placed the army on its new Imperial footing, he made the *auxilia* an integral part of it. Recruits were levied from all the provinces, except Greece, on a reasonably equitable basis. The function of this arm was to screen the less expendable legions and by operating in advance and on the flanks of the heavily armoured legionaries, take the shock of skirmishes and enemy surprise attacks. It consisted of three kinds of fighting units—cavalry, infantry and mounted infantry, organised in regiments of about 500 and 1,000 strong (*quingenaria* and *milliaria* respectively). The cavalry units were called wings (*alæ*) and the horsemen were divided into 16 troops (*turmæ*), each 32 strong including the troop commander (*decurio*). It appears from the writer Hyginus that a regiment double this size (*ala milliaria*) had 24 troops, each presumably 42 strong. The commander of a quingenary unit was a *praefectus*, and that of a unit a thousand strong a *tribunus*; both were usually young men of equestrian status for whom this appointment was a step in their social and political career.

The infantry units were organised in cohorts, with centuries, like those of the legions, 80 strong. Many of the cohorts in Britain were mounted infantry (*equitatæ*) but only a proportion of the unit was actually mounted. Hyginus tells us that a *cohors quingenaria* consisted of 380 infantry and 120 cavalry arranged in centuries and troops respectively but the details are not clear.

An example of an *ala quingenaria* was the *Ala Hispanorum Vettonum civium Romanorum*, stationed in the time of Trajan at Brecon Gaer in central Wales. This regiment was originally raised in N.W. Spain and the men serving in it at that time had received the grant of Roman citizenship. Thereafter *civium Romanorum* was its title of honour. The auxiliaries, normally recruited in the frontier provinces, were not necessarily Roman citizens before enlistment but received this status, if they did not already possess it, when they were honourably discharged after 25 or more years' service.

Other units known to have been stationed in Wales include *Cohors II Asturum equitata* (originally raised in Spain) at Llanio, and *Cohors I Nerviorum* (from a Gallic tribe made famous by Cæsar's description of their military prowess) at Cær Gai. Some units were trained and equipped for special employment—for example *Cohors I Hamiorum Sagittariorum*, a battalion of Syrian archers, in the second century stationed successively on the two Walls.

4. *The Navy* was always a useful but inferior arm and never developed as an independent force like the British Royal Navy. Its main duties were the suppression of piracy and the transportation of men and supplies. There were a number of fleets, some operating on large rivers like the Rhine and Danube. However the British fleet (*Classis Britannica*) had a more important role in the defence of Rome's major overseas province, and had a number of bases on the British and North French coasts. Its headquarters in Britain may have been Dover, and in Gaul was Boulogne.

5. *Numeri* and *Cunei* were irregular units of infantry and cavalry respectively, probably on a lower establishment than the cohorts and *alæ*, often drawn from a markedly less civilised stratum of the frontier population and probably neither so highly trained nor so well paid. Such units were initially raised for specific campaigns, but *numeri* became regular units of the army from the Hadrianic period. One of the most interesting of these units attested in Britain is the *Numerus Barcariorum Tigrisiensium* stationed in succession at Lancaster and at South Shields. This unit from the Tigris, the result of Severus's ephemeral conquests in Parthia, was evidently used for operating the military ferries across the mouth of the Tyne and in Morecambe Bay, where wide, shallow estuaries produce conditions similar to those on the Tigris. The *Numeri* were sometimes commanded by their own native leaders and their equipment remained un-Romanised. An example of the *cuneus* is the *Cuneus Frisiorum*, a member of which dedicated an altar (A.D. 222-235) at Housesteads on the Wall where the unit was presumably stationed.

I

THE LEGIONS IN BRITAIN

THE original field force which landed on the coast of Kent in A.D. 43 included four legions, the IInd *Augusta* from *Argentoratum* (Strasbourg), the XXth from *Novæsium* (Neuss), the IXth *Hispana* from Pannonia and the XIVth *Gemina* from *Moguntiacum* (Mainz) ; with auxiliary infantry and cavalry, the total expeditionary force must have comprised at least 40,000 men and Claudius, on his brief visit, was accompanied by further reinforcements, including a detachment of the Prætorian Guard.

After the initial campaign which culminated in the occupation of the British capital at *Camulodunum* (Colchester), the movements of the legions are not clear. It seems that the army was divided into several columns. The IXth struck north, part of the legion in all probability being established at a 30-acre fortress on the River Nene at Longthorpe near Peterborough. Another legion, the IInd *Augusta*, under its commander, the future Emperor Vespasian, advanced along the south coast mopping up the great string of hill fortresses in Wessex. One of these must have been Maiden Castle, where excavations have revealed a Belgic war cemetery. There, in shallow graves lay the hastily buried warriors, one of whom had still a Roman artillery bolt firmly wedged in his backbone (*Maiden Castle Excavation Report*, pl. lviii). A legionary cohort and half a quingenary *ala* of auxiliary cavalry occupied part of the hill fort on Hod Hill, and possibly another legionary detachment was stationed on Ham Hill at this time or soon afterwards.

Of the other two legions nothing certain is known. It is possible that the XXth remained as a reserve unit at Colchester where the tombstone of Facilis, the centurion, is evidence of its presence. The XIVth probably became established in the Midlands, possibly somewhere on the line of the Fosse Way. This remarkable road appears to have been the first frontier laid out by Aulus Plautius in accordance with the peace settlement made by Claudius with the British tribes. It is unfortunate that the relevant book of Tacitus, which would give us the historical background, is missing.

Very soon new dispositions became necessary. The Silures from South Wales caused trouble along the frontier and invaded Roman territory. To deal with this situation the new governor, Ostorius

Scapula, moved forward to contain the tribe within its own lands. The implication of a difficult passage of Tacitus is that a legion was detached from the base camp (the XXth from Colchester ?) and used against the Silures. This would explain the presence at Wotton near Gloucester of an early tombstone of this legion and it is possible that the fortress on the Kingsholm site at Gloucester, the important crossing of the Severn, was established by the XXth, while the IInd *Augusta* was still occupied in holding down the tribes in the south-west. At the same time the XIVth was moved along Watling Street probably to Wall, near Lichfield. The precise line of the new frontier has not yet been determined: it is possible that part of the Fosse Way from High Cross, Leicester or Margidunum was maintained.

The XIVth was used by Veranius in his Welsh campaign in A.D. 58 and moved up to Wroxeter where its presence is testified by two tombstones. Its fortress has now been found under the later city. At one time it was considered that Wroxeter was a double legionary fortress on the evidence of the single tombstone of a soldier of the XXth, but he was a *beneficiarius* of the governor, an official more likely than any other to have been on detached duty away from his legion. It seems clear that while the main sources of trouble lay in Wales, the legionary forces were concentrated on or near the western frontier; as soon as the centre of unrest moved to Brigantia, there would be a corresponding change of dispositions.

In A.D. 60, Paullinus, pursuing the new policy of the occupation of Wales, launched his initial attack on Anglesey which had become the centre of Druidism, a religion of nationalistic fervour and a rallying point of the anti-Roman feeling in Britain. The whole of the XIVth and a considerable part of the XXth were engaged while the other two legions remained in their fortresses. It is little wonder that Queen Boudicca chose this moment for her revolt (D. R. Dudley and Graham Webster, *The Rebellion of Boudicca*, 1962). Her decision was justified by events—a detachment of the IXth was cut to pieces in a gallant attempt to save the Colchester colonists and London and *Verulamium* (St. Albans) fell before the avenging Britons. It was a critical moment for the Romans, and under a less able or resolute general there might well have been an overwhelming disaster, to rank with that of Varus in Germany in A.D. 9. Fortunately for the Romans, the Brigantes remained faithful to their treaty obligations. But Paullinus faced a great horde of confident Britons with a comparatively small force, the IInd having failed to joined him at the rendezvous somewhere in the Midlands. For the subsequent victory the XIVth and XXth both received the additional title *Victrix*. By A.D. 66 the situation in Britain was so calm that the XIVth was withdrawn, and was probably replaced at Wroxeter by the XXth. At about the same time a fortress was built at Gloucester on the site later occupied by the *colonia*, presumably for the IInd; the IXth had by this period been concentrated at Lincoln.

By A.D. 71 the position in Britain had changed radically; with the seizure of the Brigantian throne by Venutius, who was bitterly opposed to the Romans, the long peace with this powerful northern tribe was at an end. To deal with the new situation, Vespasian sent to Britain Petillius Cerialis the self-same general who, in command of the IXth, had attempted to suppress the Boudiccan revolt. At the same time the provincial army was reinforced with a new legion, the IInd *Adiutrix*, raised in A.D. 69 from marines of the Adriatic fleet.

The XXth at this time was under the command of Gn. Julius Agricola and, from his biography by Tacitus, it is known that he saw service in the northern campaign. The main plan of conquest seems to have been for two columns to move into Brigantia. The eastern route up the Ouse valley into the Yorkshire Plain was taken by the IXth while the new legion, IInd *Adiutrix*, occupied the Lincoln fortress. The western route was probably taken by the XXth under Agricola, the two legions converging eventually near Stanwick where Venutius had concentrated his troops and allies. The campaign was concluded but no details have survived ; Brigantia was probably harried and occupied more thoroughly by Cerialis than Tacitus would have us believe, since the historian seems to minimize the achievements of Cerialis in order to enhance those of Agricola.

The next governor, Frontinus, completed the subjugation of Wales and moved the IInd *Augusta* from Gloucester to its permanent base of *Isca* (Caerleon) near Newport in Monmouthshire. His successor, Agricola, undertook the conquest of northern England and much of Scotland, taking with him his old legion, the XXth, which he established at Inchtuthil in Perthshire, on the great high-way which cut across the mouths of the Highland glens. This legion however maintained its base at Wroxeter, but the gap in North Wales was now filled by moving the IInd *Adiutrix* to Chester. York had already been established in 71 by Cerialis. The three permanent legionary fortresses of the province, Caerleon, York and Chester, were therefore founded within a few years of each other in the reign of Vespasian.

This arrangement for the defence of Britain suffered drastic reorganization when the Romans decided to withdraw from Scotland and establish a frontier on the Tyne-Solway line. This decision was based on the reports that Scotland had little to offer in the shape of mineral wealth and its people were hardly likely to make peaceful citizens. At the same time Domitian, requiring troops for his campaign against the Dacians, withdrew the IInd *Adiutrix* and some *auxilia*, and the XXth fell back to Chester. The establishment of a land frontier on the Tyne-Solway line was the final outcome of this plan of withdrawal and consolidation. Later developments showed that it would have been wiser to have used the shorter Clyde-Forth line but it was evidently considered at the time that this would require too many troops in garrison behind it.

About A.D. 120 the IXth *Hispana* was withdrawn, probably for service in the East. Its place was taken by the VIth, which remained in Britain with the other two legions until the end of the occupation. The only other known alteration to these dispositions, apart from garrison duties on the two Walls, was the transfer of a detachment of the IInd *Augusta* at the end of the third century, to the Saxon Shore fort of Richborough, the site of the initial invasion base in A.D. 43.

II

ORGANIZATION OF THE LEGION

THE legion of the Roman Army was, from its very inception at the dawn of the Republic, a self-contained formation equivalent to a complete army in itself. Its smallest unit was the section of eight men (*contubernium* or tent-party) who shared a tent and a pack-horse to carry it. In barracks they shared a pair of rooms for their equipment and sleeping quarters respectively. Ten of these groups formed a company (*centuria*) commanded by a centurion. The original unit undoubtedly had a hundred men but the actual strength, under active service conditions in the field, was normally 80. Six centuries, grouped in three pairs—a relic of the Republican maniple—formed a cohort and ten cohorts made up a legion. The first cohort, however, was increased in the early Principate to about double the size of the others. It consisted of five centuries, a total of 800 men picked for their physique and fighting qualities.

The legion had a total fighting strength of about 5,300 infantry but its total establishment was 6,000. It included a squadron of mounted men, 120 strong, for use as orderlies or despatch riders rather than as cavalry ; they were not organized in *turmæ* but were carried on the books of the various centuries.

Ten

Th e Officers.

The legion, together with any attached auxiliary units, was commanded by a *legatus*, a senator who had served as *prætor* and was commonly a man in his thirties. The normal duration of the appointment was three years. Under him were six military tribunes—one was a young man of high birth, intended for a senatorial career, serving for two or three years as *tribunus laticlavius* before reaching the age of 25 and entering the senate as *quæstor*. His main task was to learn the art of generalship in order to qualify himself, in another ten years' time or so, for a legionary legateship. The other five tribunes were of equestrian rank and described as *tribuni angusticlavii*. Most of them were men in their thirties or upwards whose previous experience had been mainly as municipal magistrates. Many of them, especially from the time of Hadrian, had previously served as prefects of auxiliary cohorts and might hope to proceed to the prefecture of an *ala*, and thereafter, if sufficiently well thought of by the Emperor's advisers, to enter the upper grades of the administrative service as a procurator. The five *tribuni angusticlavii* were employed as staff officers at legionary headquarters but on a campaign they might on occasions find themselves in command of detachments.

The senior professional officer in the legion was the Camp Prefect (*præfectus castrorum*), responsible generally for its internal organization, training and equipment. He was a former chief centurion, normally a man of 30 years' service or more. The backbone of the army was undoubtedly the corps of centurions, 60 to each legion (pl. Ic). They were the officers immediately responsible for training and leading the centuries which they commanded. The majority of them had risen from the ranks of the legion, in some cases after serving as centurions or decurions in the *auxilia*. Others were commissioned after serving in the ranks of the guard (*evocati*), and a smaller proportion received direct commissions from civilian life. The senior centurions (*primi ordines*) served in the first cohort. At their head, commanding the first century, was the Chief Centurion (*primus pilus*) a man of at least 50, but lucky if he reached that exalted position before the age of 60. Next to him came the *princeps* who had particular responsibility for all the book-keeping and office work of the legion, in addition to training and tactical duties. A centurion who obtained promotion to *primus pilus* held that post for one year and then received a large gratuity ; he might then retire from the army but if fit and willing to continue in the Emperor's service, he was, as *primipilaris*, eligible for a wide variety of responsible and well-paid posts in the equestrian service. Whereas the ordinary soldier (*miles*) could expect retirement after his normal service term, the centurions were only discharged when they were no longer fit for their posts.

Each century of eighty men, the smallest administrative unit, was commanded by a centurion under whom was an *optio* (pl. Ia), so called since originally the centurion nominated his own second-in-command. An *optio* who had been accepted for promotion to the centurionate and was awaiting a vacancy was known as an *optio ad spem ordinis*. Each century had a *signifer* or standard bearer, a man picked no doubt for his appearance and bearing, but also acting as treasurer of the soldiers' burial club and voluntary savings bank. A junior officer in each century was the *tesserarius*, who took command of small pickets and fatigue parties and was responsible for receiving the watchword. The cohort was a tactical rather than an administrative unit except, of course, when it was operating as an independent *vexillatio* or detachment.

The situation at headquarters level was very complicated, since there were large numbers of specialist officers accorded privileges such as exemption from fatigues and hence classified as *immunes*. The actual staff of clerks and orderlies forming the *tabularium legionis* in headquarters was under the command of the *cornicularius* (adjutant) assisted by an *actuarius*, an office which came into being under Severus and became increasingly important as he was responsible for collecting the *annona* or corn tax from the provincials. The office became eventually a purely civil one and its holders were, in the late Empire, a byword on account of their sharp practices. There were several kinds of *librarii* (clerks) and *exacti* (literally, one who exacts payment, equivalent to the modern accountant). The clerks included those who kept records of the granaries which housed the staple food of the legion (*horreorum librarii*) and those who operated the compulsory savings bank into which half the imperial donatives were paid and became available to the soldier only on discharge (*librarii depositorum*). The wills and properties of those killed on active service were looked after by the *librarii caducorum*.

The senior officer below the rank of centurion was the *aquilifer*, the standard bearer who carried the silver eagle, the most sacred symbol of the legion (pl. Ib). Below him was the *imaginifer*, another standard bearer who carried the image of the Emperor. Under these officers came the various buglers and trumpeters who sounded the commands and used three kinds of instrument. The main commands given by the commander-in-chief were transmitted to the standard bearers by the *cornicines* who had large circular instruments of horn and bronze. They were also present at the sacrifices and sounded their horns to drive away evil spirits. When the Emperor appeared a special fanfare, the *classicum*, was played. At a lower level commands were given by the *tubicen*, a soldier who carried a *tuba*, a long, bell-mouthed bronze instrument somewhat akin to the modern bugle. This was used also at military funerals. The third type was the *bucina* carried by a *bucinator*. This instrument was named after a twisted shell and may originally have been copied from this. The military *bucina* appears to have been curved as well as twisted and was used to sound the watches.

The commander and the tribunes each had their own orderlies, these being clerks rather than personal servants, who would have been slaves. These orderlies or *beneficiarii* took precedence from the rank of their officer. Those attached to the Governor's staff, on secondment from their legion, could have responsible posts as toll collectors and district officers.

There were many specialist craftsmen as one would expect in a unit which was responsible for engineering construction on a large scale. The *architectus* was the master builder, the *mensor* the surveyor who set out the camp lines. The *hydraularius* was responsible for water supply and drainage. There was a large number of craftsmen named after their trade such as *naupegus* (shipwright), *ballistarius* (catapult maker), *specularius* (glazier), *sagittarius* (arrow maker), the woodsmen in charge of tree felling, and many others.

The religious ceremonies and sacrifices were organized by the *haruspices* (priests or soothsayers) who had charge over the *victimarii* (sacrificial assistants). One scene from Trajan's Column (pl. VIId) shows the long procession moving round the fort with the animals, in order of importance. By the altar and the veiled priest stand the *cornicines* with their horns under their arms.

An important aspect of army organization was the medical service. It was realized that highly-trained soldiers could not be allowed to die from wounds on the battlefield, for want of attention. The health of the legionaries depended to a great extent on physical fitness, personal cleanliness and a plain, wholesome diet. The last consisted of cheese and vegetables and of corn made into porridge or bread; meat was eaten only occasionally but on an increasing scale from the first century, when pork had preference. The legionaries drank quantities of a rough wine imported from Gaul and Spain in the large *amphoræ*, fragments of which are often found on Roman sites in Britain. Each unit had a medical officer (the *medicus ordinarius*, equal in rank to a centurion) who was often a Greek, like Hermogenes and Antiochus, who set up altars at Chester. Under this officer were medical orderlies (*medici*) and dressers (*capsarii*), named from the bandage bag (*capsa*) they carried in the field. On Trajan's Column there is a very graphic illustration of a field dressing station, showing an auxiliary having a dressing applied to a wound in his thigh (pl. VIIIb). Hospitals (*valetudinaria*) were attached to many camps and forts, where the sick and wounded could be segregated and treated. Knowledge of medicines and drugs was elementary and highly empirical. Nevertheless, natural antiseptics such as pitch and turpentine were employed and much use was made of herbal lore which has, regrettably, been lost with the development of modern pharmacy. A number of ancient treatises on medicine and surgery have survived which throw much light on methods used in classical times. Celsus (*De Medicina*) deals with surgery and makes it clear that simple operations were commonplace and there are many examples of implements being found, some of them of a complex character. For army doctors, extraction of foreign bodies and amputations were the commonest requirements. Here knowledge and skill were considerable and the descriptions of operations of this character, by Paul of Aegina, have a modern ring.

III

THE LEGION IN THE FIELD

THE Romans relied not only on sound training and discipline, but also on thorough preparations ; plans for every campaign and battle were carefully thought out beforehand and little was left to chance. The personalities of different commanders naturally created variations : Vespasian, in whose service the Jewish historian Josephus was able to follow the course of the Jewish War, was a very cautious general and his successes were the result of the wearing down of his opponents by a steady and relentless pressure rather than any brilliant strokes of military genius. The Romans occasionally produced great generals like Cæsar and Corbulo but their speed of movement and sense of tactical initiative were exceptional. The Romans knew full well that victory lay with " the big battalions ", with splendidly trained and equipped soldiers, a well organized commissariat, proper consolidation of gains and, above all, a sense of destiny and purpose and a feeling of natural superiority over their barbarian foes.

There are several different sources from which information can be derived about military operations and tactics. Perhaps the best description of a Roman army at war is given by Josephus, who had the advantage of seeing it at close hand from both aspects, those of an enemy and an ally of the Romans, having at first fought against them but, after being captured, won over to their service. Their success is due, he says, to the firm discipline, constant drill and battle practice by which they became hardened to war and skilled in the use of new weapons. He, like Vegetius, was impressed by their discipline and order in the camp—" . . . they live together by companies with quietness and decency, as are all their other affairs managed with good order and security. Each company hath also their wood and their corn and their water, brought them when they stand in need of them ; for they neither sup nor dine as they please themselves singly, but all together. Their times also for sleeping and watching, and rising, are notified beforehand by the sound of trumpets, nor is any thing done without such a signal ; . . ." (Whiston's translation). They march quietly and " every one keeps his own rank ". Later he describes the army on the march in detail. First went the auxiliary cavalry, advancing as a screen in the front and flanks to prevent any surprise attack. All woods and places where the enemy might hide were carefully searched. Then marched the auxiliary infantry followed by the engineers and surveyors responsible for setting out the camp. Behind them were the road constructors ready to go ahead and deal with any obstruc- tion, then the carts and wagons of the supply train, guarded by cavalry. Following this train came the commander with his bodyguard, in front of the legionary cavalry, then the siege train and heavy artillery, and finally the legions in ranks six deep behind their standards and trumpeters, with the centurions marching in the rear. Straggling behind were the camp followers with the baggage, borne by mules, and finally a strong rearguard of auxiliary infantry and cavalry. Josephus tells us that before marching away they set fire to the camp to prevent the enemy from using it. There would, however, be very little to burn in a tented camp except the palisade and timber towers on the ramparts, and perhaps it was these which the Romans destroyed.

Tactics varied with the nature of the enemy and the terrain, but in open warfare the core of the fighting force was the body of legionaries. Between them and the enemy until the actual moment of contact was a screen of cavalry, slingers, archers and light artillery. The enemy was thus engaged from a distance by methods which they could not often use themselves.

The cavalry arm was composed of auxiliary units like the light Gallic and Moorish horsemen. Their main task in the first and second centuries, apart from general reconnaissance, was chasing disorganized enemy forces in flight and intercepting infiltration or outflanking movements. Heavy cavalry, used as shock troops, was not employed until the third century when it became necessary to develop a mobile arm of this nature to break up large barbarian concentrations attempting to cross the frontiers. The legions then became garrison troops holding key positions at points of strategic importance. The small force of legionary cavalry, only 120 in the first century but later increased, was used for scouting and conveying despatches.

Long-range missiles, such as sling-stones, arrows and bolts, were used both against defended positions and in pitched battles. Slingers and stone throwers were used extensively in ancient warfare and some of the most skilled came from the Balearic Islands; their ammunition consisted of lead bullets (*glandes plumba*) or round stones about the size of a fist which they could project with great velocity and considerable accuracy. These troops, lightly armed, operated on the flanks and directed their fire at the point of attack. Against a defended position, they were useful in keeping the defenders under cover while the legionaries closed up to their final assault positions.

Archers were similarly used. Their weapon was a small bow of great strength, cunningly made of strips of wood and bone. Most of the best archers came from the east—it was the mounted Parthian archers who had been such a menace to the Roman infantry in one of the early eastern wars. Their steel-tipped arrows, fired with great rapidity and velocity, had pierced the legionaries' body armour.

The legions were equipped with two kinds of spring-operated artillery, the light field-gun or *carroballista* and the large catapult, the *onager*. The former could be mounted on a small cart drawn by two ponies. A detachment of ten men operated this gun, one of which was issued to each century. These sixty field-guns could lay down a barrage of arrows or iron bolts about nine inches long. Against native encampments, the bolts were bound with tar-coated tow and set alight before firing. The effect on enemy morale can well be imagined, as, with their homes blazing behind them, they faced the rapidly advancing legionaries. Against prepared positions the guns were mounted on log platforms to give extra height. The large catapults (*onagri*), one of which was operated by each cohort, were very powerful and could hurl a large boulder weighing two hundredweights a distance of 400-500 yards. In Roman forts large *ballistæ* were usually mounted at the corners where the turf rampart was laced with logs and brushwood to increase its resilience.

The actual battle in the open was decided by the hand-to-hand clash of armed men, in which a great deal depended on taking the best advantage of terrain. Many ruses were adopted to gain the upper hand. Commanders sought to give their forces moral superiority before and during the battle. Some examples of this are given by Frontinus in his *Strategemata*. For example, Marcus Marcellus in 216 B.C., fearing that a feeble battle cry would reveal the small number of his forces, ordered all the camp followers, cooks and slaves, to join in the cry. Another useful idea was to make the enemy and one's own troops think that reinforcements were arriving. Papirius Cursor, fighting the Samnites, arranged for some horsemen to race their animals down a nearby hill, trailing branches behind them. The resulting dust-cloud heartened the Romans and caused panic in the Samnite ranks. Sometimes the same effect was gained by accident. At the battle of Cremona in the Civil War of A.D. 69, the Rhineland legions gathered together by Vitellius and composed of Gauls and Germans, were facing the troops under Vespasian from the east. After an all-night indecisive struggle, the sun rose and the IIIrd Legion, recruited from the near East, in its usual style turned and saluted it. This gesture was misunderstood by the Vitellian army, who thought that Vespasian's legionaries were hailing reinforcements. They broke and fled and Italy and Rome lay open to the Flavian forces.

Surprise attacks in the rear and flank were also common but only successful against inexperienced or badly led troops. Similarly the enemy could sometimes be lured into an ambush by pretended flight ; this simple manœuvre has been decisive in many critical battles. One of the greatest disasters to Roman arms, the total loss of three legions under Varus, was inflicted by the wily German chieftain Arminius, who drew the Roman army into an ambush in the depths of the Teutoburg Forest.

On the frontiers, as in Britain, the Romans had to deal with ill-organized and badly-equipped natives whose only advantages lay in their courage, intensified by a desire not to succumb to Roman thraldom, and in their intimate knowledge of the terrain. If they were wise, they avoided a pitched battle, since here the discipline and armour of the legionary was always the decisive factor. Usually the native fought a fierce delaying action in the guerilla style, harassing lines of communication and falling savagely on any small force of Romans which became detached from the main body. In difficult country the Romans found this kind of warfare heavy going and expensive. Domitian's campaign against the Chatti in the wilds of the Taunus was just such a war. Frontinus tells us how the Chatti took refuge in the forest and how difficult it was for the Roman cavalry to operate against them. To deal with this problem, Domitian ordered the horsemen to dismount and fight on foot (*Strategemata*, II, iii, 23).

In Britain, the campaigns were marked by a number of pitched battles and assaults but there were doubtless many fierce guerilla campaigns in the Welsh mountains and the bleak Pennines. In the great battle which completed the conquest of Scotland at *Mons Graupius*, Agricola used his auxiliaries, and held the legions in reserve. This may have been by necessity but it clearly demonstrates how by then the *auxilia* had proved themselves and how the Romans had begun at last to appreciate the value of cavalry. The legions still had their part to play but their days as crack fighting units were numbered.

It was in siege tactics that the Roman army showed the peak of its achievements, both in organization and equipment. Its pre-eminence in this direction caused Frontinus in his introduction to Book III to lapse into a rash prophecy : " I will first submit," he says, " those (stratagems) which are useful in the siege of cities, then those which offer suggestions to the besieged. Laying aside also all considerations of works and engines of war, the invention of which has long since reached its limit and for the improvement of which I see no further hope in the applied arts . . ."

There is little doubt that the Romans had brought siege craft to a fine art and rarely was a garrison able to hold out for long against them. If a fortress could not be taken by direct assault, the army settled down to place a stranglehold on it. This was achieved by circumvallation, i.e., a ditch system cut right round the enemy stronghold to prevent any communication being received from the outside world. Mighty siege engines were then brought forward to batter down the defences. An almost continuous artillery barrage was maintained to prevent the enemy on the ramparts from interfering with this progress. One of the best examples of these tactics, which is at the same time a graphic piece of writing, comes from the pen of Josephus in his description of the siege of Jotapata in the Jewish War of A.D. 68.

Jotapata was a place of great natural strength, three sides being protected by precipices ; only on the north was there an even approach. The Romans first surrounded the city to cut it off completely from the surrounding country. Having rested his forces after their strenuous mountain march, Vespasian tried a direct assault ; the main attacking party manœuvred into position under the cover of a withering barrage from archers and slingers. The Jews then sallied forth and with great spirit drove the Romans back. Further fighting of a similar nature took place on five succeeding days until at length the Romans were able to reach the city walls.

Then the besieging troops began to erect sloping banks to gain the wall tops. To protect the soldiers who were bringing up the earth and stones in baskets, large hurdles were erected along the edges of the bank. At the same time the Romans brought up their heavy artillery and 160 catapults were placed at points of vantage to keep the defenders under constant fire. Not only stones (weighing a talent, i.e., about 60 lbs.) but arrows and fire darts were used. The Jews tried desperate sallies, tearing down the hurdles to attack the unprotected workers behind, but fully armoured units were sent forward to intercept these raiders. As the banks grew higher and nearer to the top of the walls, the Jews began to quail but Josephus ordered the walls to be raised and, to protect his workmen, erected screens of raw oxhides ; they also increased the height of their towers to outrange the Roman artillery. Vespasian now determined on a long-term plan of starving the Jews with the intention of renewing the assault when the garrison was weakened by famine. The besieged, however, had plenty of food but lacked water, having no wells, and this precious commodity had to be rationed. When the Romans became aware of this they were greatly heartened but Josephus resorted to a trick to cause the Romans to obtain a different impression of the critical state of affairs. He ordered that wet cloths be hung over the battlements. This was a variation of the old stratagem used by the Romans themselves who, when besieged in their capital by the Gauls and reduced to sorry straits of starvation, threw bread at their enemy and so discouraged them that the siege held until relief came. Vespasian appears to have been deceived by this trick for he renewed a close assault, this time bringing a massive battering ram to bear on a part of the wall. This massive beam was slung on cradles so that its iron head in the shape of a ram rhythmically battered at the same point, until a hole was made sufficient to enable the engineers to undermine the wall. The men who operated the ram were protected by close set hurdles forming a substantial roof over them. To counteract the effect of this engine, the Jews lowered sacks of chaff between the ram and the wall but the Romans tied sharp hooks to long poles and cut the ropes. The Jews then made a desperate sally, threw pitch on the machine and set it on fire ; also a certain Jew " took up a stone of vast bigness " and threw it down on the ram's head with such force that it broke it off. During these engagements an arrow pierced Vespasian's foot and exaggerated rumour flew from mouth to mouth producing great consternation in the Roman ranks. The personal leadership of a great general meant much to these armies and frequently the battle was lost when the commander was slain. As soon as it was discovered that the wound was not serious, the Romans renewed the struggle with greater vigour than ever, determined to avenge this blow. A critical stage was now reached and the barrage from the catapults and other machines was worked up to a crescendo all night, prior to the storming of the walls. At dawn, the troops crept up into their assault positions with their ladders ; at the blast of a trumpet the whole army gave a great shout, every archer, slinger and engine poured a single volley into the defenders of the walls to cover the forward movement. Josephus had prepared for this. Placing his strongest men in the breaches, he ordered everyone to stop up their ears so as not to be alarmed at the great shout and all were to crouch under their shields while the great volley was discharged, then to rise and fling themselves at the assault parties. A long and bitter struggle ensued. The Romans maintained and increased their pressure by throwing reinforcements into the battle against the flagging defenders. The legionaries advancing along the wall front protected themselves by forming a *testudo* (pl. VIIIa). This familiar device consisted of interlocking shields held over the heads of the legionaries. It was proof against most missiles but the Jews poured boiling oil on them from the battlements, which penetrated the shields and ran under the armour, causing bad burns and intense pain. They also threw blazing fat on to the boards forming the incline, which made them very slippery and difficult to climb. Such was the ingenuity and courage of the Jews that the assault faltered and in the evening the troops were called off. Vespasian now ordered the banks to be raised to a higher level but amid the bustle of renewed activity, a surprise attack was planned. A deserter had reported that the Jews were in a wearied condition and that the night watch was ill-kept. A small body, under Vespasian's son Titus, quietly assembled in the middle of the night and, placing their ladder against the wall, took the guards by surprise. They rushed the citadel in the town and gained control. With the enemy in their midst, the defenders panicked and the main body of the Roman army was able to force its way through the defences. The strenuous siege of 47 days, with its bitter memories, left no feeling of mercy in Roman hearts. The whole of the 40,000 inhabitants, except infants and women, were put to the sword or hurled down the precipice. How Josephus escaped and lived to write this grim story is another matter. This shortened account serves to illustrate siege tactics of both attackers and defenders.

The fortresses of Britain did not cause the Romans such trouble as Jotapata and most of them must have fallen by direct assault, but unfortunately little is known. Tacitus tells us about the attack on the stronghold in central Wales where Caratacus had assembled his forces. The legionaries were at first aghast at the apparent strength of this hill fortress built on a precipitous slope but, rallied by their leaders, they climbed the rugged slopes and gained the ramparts at the first attempt. Once inside the defences, their double-edged swords made short work of the Welsh tribesmen.

Signalling.

Despatches were sent by horsemen and mainly for this purpose each legion was equipped with 120 cavalry. Although pigeons are mentioned by Frontinus, it is clear that this was a special case and these birds were not normally used for conveying messages. By the end of the first century, the Romans had developed a system of signalling by means of smoke in the day and fires at night, adopted doubtless from the Parthians, where desert conditions made their use very effective. On Trajan's Column there are wooden signal towers with small haycocks and carefully built log platforms. Richmond distinguishes several types of signal stations from the fortlets on the north coast of Devon of the first century to the elaborate stone structures on the Yorkshire coast of the late fourth century (*The Archaeology of Roman Britain*, 2nd edition (1969), 60). The remains of signal stations are so slight that they have for the most part escaped notice in Britain. Aerial reconnaissance is gradually bringing them to light and it is becoming obvious that the whole of northern Britain in Roman times was covered with a network of these signal stations so that messages could be passed rapidly for great distances from the forward stations to base head-quarters. An example of this system in the Stainmore Pass has been described where carefully sited signal stations provided rapid " telegraphic " communication between Hadrian's Wall and Command Headquarters at York (I. A. Richmond in *Aspects of Archæology*). Details of methods by which signals were sent are not known but there may have been a code involving several fires or smoke columns with the possibility of a number of combinations being observed from a distance. It would have been a simple matter to have held a covering over one or more of the smoke columns in the fashion of the North American Indians and, by this means, a letter code could have been used and not merely signals but words spelt out over the system. Vegetius (iii. 5) says that fire, smoke and semaphore codes were used and Polybius, as early as the Punic Wars, described a rather cumbersome method of using torches held aloft for a specified length of time and gives an improvised system of his own using a letter code (x, 44).

Most writers agree that the success of the Roman Army was largely due to the stiff discipline imposed on all ranks. Discipline is the root of morale, a fact not always appreciated by the rankers, and is obtained by personal smartness and unit drill. There is little doubt that high standards were laid down in the legions and one can well imagine the endless parades with their emphasis on " spit and polish ". Marching, arms drill (*armatura*), weapon training and tactical exercises were all strenuously undertaken. Josephus tells us that the soldiers did not begin to use their weapons first in time of war but fought as if their weapons " did always cling to them—they have never any truce from warlike exercises. . . . every soldier is every day exercised and that with real diligence, as if it were in time of war, which is the reason why they bear the fatigue of battle so easily, for neither can any disorder remove them from their usual regularity, nor can fear affright them out of it, nor can labour tire them : which firmness of conduct makes them always to overcome those that have not the same firmness, nor would he be mistaken that would call these their exercises unbloody battles and their battles bloody exercises." (Whiston's translation.)

The Army had not always been well drilled and disciplined. In the days of the Republic and early Empire, the individual commanders had been responsible for raising their troops to better standards and therein lay the importance of the personality of the general, since their armies had to be persuaded of this stern necessity and only a general with great qualities of leadership could inspire such a devotion to duty in his men. Such a man, for example, was Corbulo. When he arrived in Syria, in the reign of Nero, to undertake a campaign in Armenia, he found the army in a low state of morale. Quartered in towns instead of barracks, after years of peace, their martial qualities had been dissipated. To mould these idle and decadent soldiers to his purpose, he marched them out of Syria to winter in the bleak uplands round Lake Van. Sentries froze to death at their posts and many perished in the stiff conditions suddenly imposed, but, by spring, Corbulo had a tough fighting force with which he undertook a rapid and brilliant campaign in Greater Armenia. The effect on Roman history of Cæsar's veterans, toughened by years of hard campaigning under one of the most exacting commanders ever known, is well known. These same veterans, rallying to the cause of Cæsar's adopted son, Augustus, enabled him to fulfil his destiny. Systems of drill and tactical exercise were gradually introduced so that, by the time of Trajan, the whole army was in a state of high efficiency. This was largely achieved by the introduction of drill masters, the *lanistæ*, originally copied from the gladiatorial schools about 105 B.C.

There was also maintained a rigid code of punishment which to modern ways seems extremely harsh. The extreme penalty incurred by mutiny or desertion in the face of the enemy was death ; in the case of a unit, decimation was occasionally carried out, whereby every tenth man was executed. This practice, according to Frontinus, dated from Appius Claudius (280 B.C.) who led the Romans against Pyrrhus. Quintus Fabius Maximus (142-140 B.C.) cut off the right hands of deserters. Flogging was fairly common-place and some centurions, as Tacitus tells us (*Annals*, i. 23, 12), were not slow to use their vine staffs when occasion demanded. Other punishment consisted of demotion or degradation, loss of pay, special fatigues and a cut in rations, or having to eat barley instead of wheat. For allowing the enemy to break into his camp and set fire to the defences, Mark Antony (36 B.C.) decimated the soldiers of two cohorts responsible, dismissed the commander in disgrace and put the rest of the legion on barley rations. Sentries found asleep at their posts were usually stoned to death by their comrades since the fault was a serious failure in responsibility.

If discipline and punishment were harsh, some of the tactical exercises were equally tough. Vegetius (i. 26, 27 ; ii, 23) tells us that three times a month the infantry did route marches of ten miles, varying the pace from the normal march to a rapid trot. They were also expected to carry out extensive manœuvres to get accustomed to the usual formation movements in attack and defence. Most of their time, as one would expect, was given to arms drill and target practice, which was varied with physical training consisting of running, jumping, tree-cutting and ground clearance. An interesting inscription has survived in Africa, bearing parts of a harangue given by Hadrian before his troops, who had been engaged for several days on special exercises for the Emperor's inspection (Lewis and Rheinhold, *Roman Civilisation*, ii, No. 148). He hands out praise and criticism with equal firmness. The legion (III *Augusta*) behaved in an exemplary manner. Turning to the cavalry the Emperor declared, " You have done the most difficult thing of all, hurling javelins when in full armour".

Now, no doubt, he addresses the infantry, " the building of fortifications which others would have spread over several days, you completed in a single day ; a wall requiring much labour and of a type which is usually built for a permanent winter camp, you constructed in no greater time than it takes to build one of turf which, being cut in pieces of equal size, is both carried and handled with ease and built up without trouble as being by its own nature pliable and level ; you built your wall with huge, heavy uneven stones ... you dug a trench (*sc.* ditch) in a straight line in hard gravel and trimmed it smooth. When this work had been approved, you went into the camp, hurriedly ate a meal, sprang to arms, and followed the cavalry out " (as if into action).

Hadrian went on to commend the commander for directing this " training which has achieved a close resemblance to actual warfare." He had fault to find with the cavalry, for their movements were not executed with sufficient care. The auxiliary unit, the *Ala I Pannoniorum*, he is inclined to damn with faint praise but appears to be satisfied with their jumping and spear throwing. The *Coh. Eq. VI Commagenorum*, i.e., the mounted infantry of that part-mounted battalion, obviously did not impress the Emperor, but as he says, " the appearance of the horses and the condition of weapons bears its relation to the level of pay." However, he pats the unit on the back by intimating that they made up for their deficiencies with the energy and enthusiasm with which they worked. The discovery of a further inscription bearing the comments of the troops on this scorcher of an exercise under the hot African sun would be most revealing.

Earthworks resulting from training exercises have been identified at several places in Britain. The series of camps on the Yorkshire Moors at Cawthorn excavated by Professor Richmond (*Arch.J.* lxxxix, 17) is thought to have been made for practice and sheds much light on the methods and stages of construction. Eighteen small practice camps were surveyed in 1811 at Llandrindod Common, Radnorshire, and half of these are still visible (*Arch. Camb.*, CXVIII (1969), 124–134). The massive circumvallation round Woden Law was thought by Professor Richmond to be the result of a field exercise, and ballista platforms for target practice are known at Birrenswark (Dumfriesshire). There are probably many other examples waiting discovery and careful excavation can reveal their true nature.

IV

THE EQUIPMENT OF THE LEGIONARY

THE equipment of the legionary differed very little from one part of the Empire to the other. The offensive weapons were the sword (*gladius*) and javelin (*pilum*). The sword, which was used in close-quarter fighting, had a short, broad blade, two feet long, with a double edge. The quillons were short and thick and the pommel weighted to give effective balance. It was carried in a leather or wood scabbard with bronze fittings, which were often gilded (pl. IIb).

As all Roman ironwork was the result of hammering and tempering, the blade was very tough. The sword was carried high on the right-hand side of the body. This may at first seem cumbersome but in this position it was clear of the shield arm and did not get entangled in the legs—the fault, incidentally, of the long sword. It was drawn by the right hand after the *pila* had been discharged. The lines of closely formed legionaries advanced shoulder to shoulder with their shields almost meeting in a solid wall. In their heavy armour the legionaries could afford to get at close grips with the enemy and thrust the sword into the stomach and soft parts of the body. They did not waste their energies in any heroic swinging and hacking with this weapon. The natives against whom they fought usually wore helmets to protect them from any downstroke and the raising of the sword arm exposed the armpit, a vulnerable target for a spear. The short sword was characteristic of the confident, attacking soldier. When the Empire went over to the defensive, the long sword (*spatha*) became more widely used. This was a weapon more adapted to keep the enemy at bay or to reach him from a defensive position.

The javelin (*pilum*) was a weapon with a killing range of about 30 yards. It was seven feet long including an iron head two feet long (pl. IIa). This head was cunningly devised, only the point, square in section and varying in length from three to ten inches, being tempered; the shank was left in its soft iron state except for the lower end which was hammered out to form a socket for the attachment of the wooden shaft. When this weapon was thrown, the enemy warriors raised their shields for protection; these were pierced by the head of the javelin and the weight of the shaft bent the soft iron shank. The enemy had an awkward seven-foot encumbrance firmly fixed to his shield and in the heat of the battle with the steady advance of the legionaries, it was an instinctive action to throw the shield away, which was exactly what the Romans intended. The butt of the javelin was shod in metal, presumably for use against cavalry, when the javelins could be used as a defensive hedge. A leather thong was probably attached to the wooden shaft at the point of balance to help to throw the javelin and give it a twist, for a spinning movement would give its flight steadiness and length. It is for precisely this purpose that the modern rifle barrel is rifled.

The legionaries carried two javelins on the march but in the camp there would be stacks of these weapons on the rampart ready for instant use. For defence purposes, however, a much stouter weapon was required ; this was wholly of wood, six feet long, pointed at both ends with a piece carved out to form a central hand-grip. It is probable that these weapons had a dual function.

The iron *pilum* was a missile useless as a spear on the ramparts owing to the fragile nature of the soft iron shank. The wooden *pilum* was suitable both for thrusting the enemy from the rampart and for use like a quarterstaff. Its other function was probably to form a palisade round the camp ; one pointed end could quickly be thrust into the ground and the other would make the scaling of the fence hazardous. The central handgrip was useful for thonging the stakes together with withies or osiers. If each soldier carried two of these stakes, a rough but efficient fence could very quickly be planted on the rampart made from the upcast from the ditch which could be cut round the camp.

The short dagger (*pugio*) may have been used for " in-fighting " if the sword had been lost but it was probably more useful as a knife. This weapon was slung on the left side, where it was too small to interfere with the shield arm.

DEFENSIVE EQUIPMENT.

Two types of legionary helmet (*galea*) are found in Britain. The main difference is the projection at the back. In one case this is flat and horizontal resembling the peak of a jockey cap. There are several of these from Britain and one of them was found in the River Thames at London and is now in the British Museum (Pl.IIIa). Another, in Lewes Museum, was recovered from Bosham Harbour. It is evident that this type, in use during the invasion period, was very soon replaced by another version in which the neck guard slopes down and around the upper shoulders giving more effective protection. This is the kind of helmet found with the remains of armour associated with the Boudiccan revolt of 60 at Colchester (*Camulodunum*, Fig. 62). The helmet shown on the model in the Newstead Gallery (Pl.IIa) is this type which may have become out-moded before Chester became a legionary fortress. Most helmets have traces of plume-holders. On one recently acquired by the British Museum, there are three, one at the top and two at the sides, but they are not in line. The campaign scenes on Trajan's Column make it clear that plumes were only worn on parade and they have the appearance of small upright feathers fixed on top of the helmet. It is probable that for special occasions other plumes would be used. There is also the suggestion that horse-hair crests were used like those of the Life Guards, from the top of the helmet to the back of the neck. It is interesting to note that this later type of helmet came back into fashion in the Civil War of the 17th century when the introduction of firearms led to open warfare with lighter equipment.

Twenty-six

a. Tombstone of an optio at Chester.    b. Tombstone of an aquilifer at Mainz.   c. Tombstone of a centurion at Bonn.

a. Life-sized model of a legionary (Grosvenor Museum).

b. Sword and scabbard

(British Museum copyright).

a. *Legionary helmet*

(*British Museum copyright*).

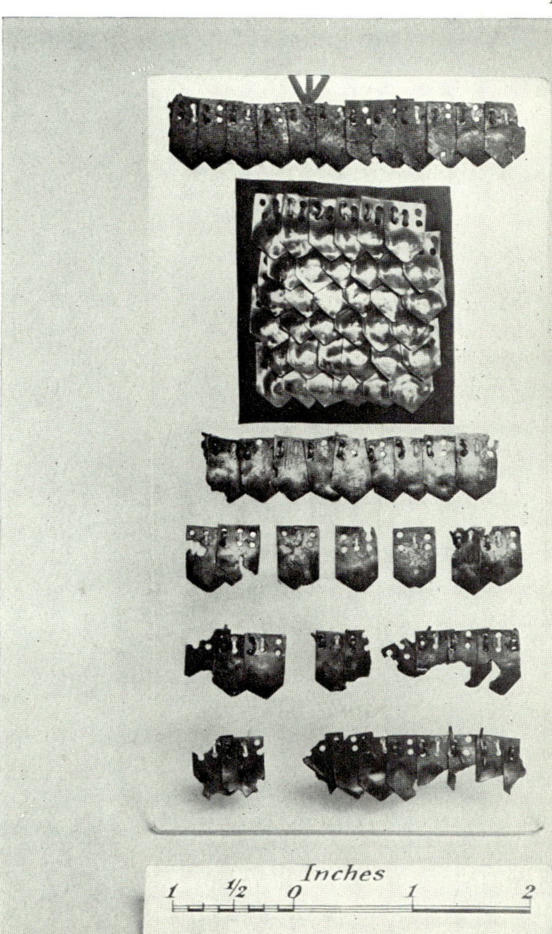

b. *Scale armour from Corbridge.*

a.   A diorama of the Chester fortress (Grosvenor Museum).

b.   Model of east gate, Chester (Grosvenor Museum).

c.   Model of Chester amphitheatre (Grosvenor Museum).

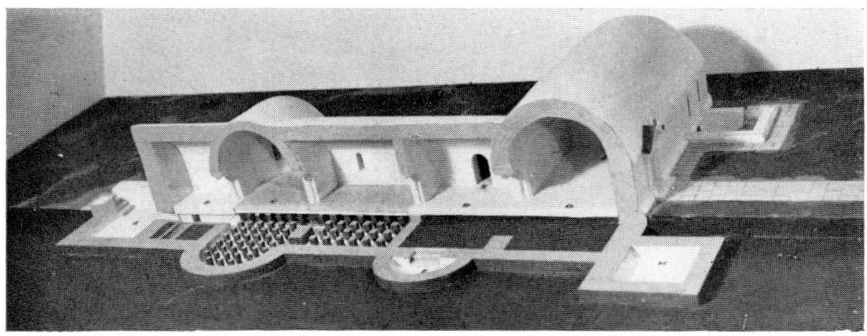

a. Model of bath-house (Grosvenor Museum).

b. Model of granaries (Grosvenor Museum).

c. Roof reconstructed from Roman materials (Grosvenor Museum).

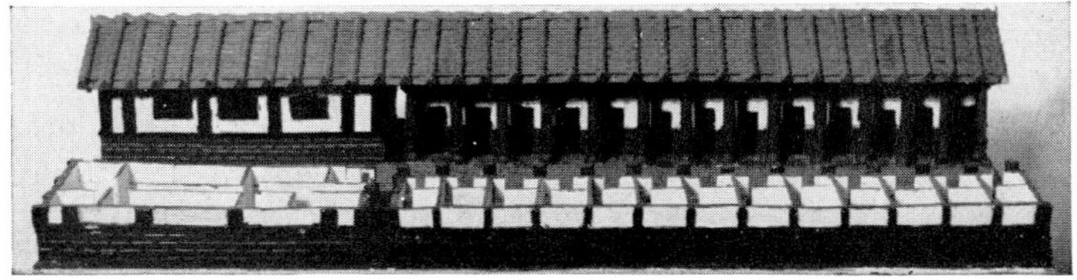

d. Model of barrack block (Grosvenor Museum).

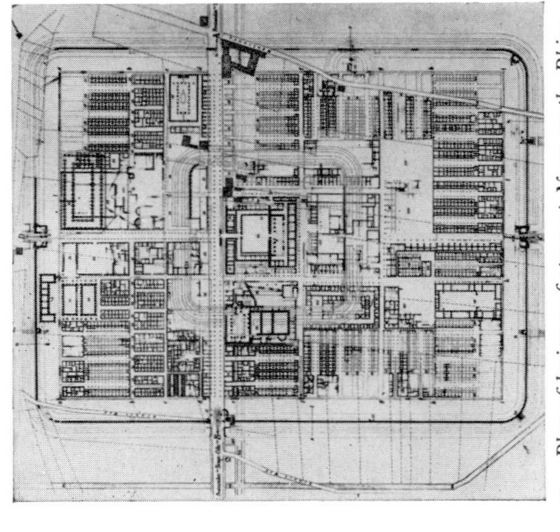

c. Plan of legionary fortress at Neuss on the Rhine.

d. Building artillery platforms for a siege.

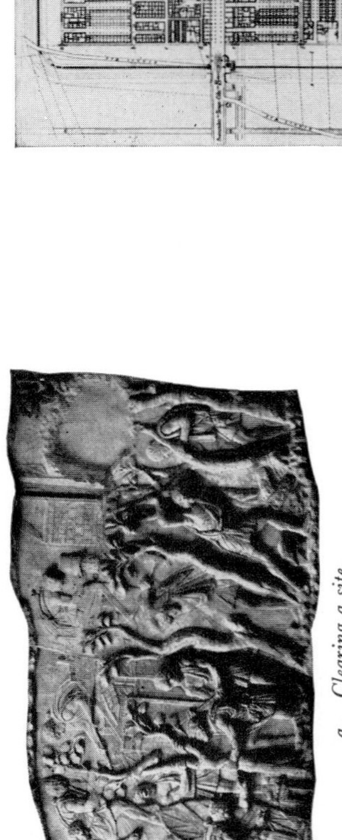

a. Clearing a site.

b. A forage party.

SCENES FROM TRAJAN'S COLUMN.

c. *The Fleet leaving harbour.*

d. *The sacrificial procession.*

a. *Soldiers loading equipment into sea-going transports.*

b. *Legionaries crossing a bridge.*

SCENES FROM TRAJAN'S COLUMN.

c. The enemy cavalry crossing a river.

d. The front line.

a. The testudo and Trajan on a tribunal.

b. A field dressing station and mobile artillery.

SCENES FROM TRAJAN'S COLUMN.

There were three types of body armour, well illustrated on the base of the Antonine Column in the scene depicting Marcus Aurelius delivering an *allocutio* or harangue. The most common form at the time of Trajan was the *lorica segmentata*. This consisted of two parts, a flexible system of overlapping metal strips and two pairs of plates over the chest and back. The body portion of strips was held together by leather thongs at the back, and fastened at the front with hooks and laces (or straps and buckles in some cases). As is shown on Trajan's Column the plates were fastened together loosely enough to enable the soldier to move and bend with ease. The upper half of the *lorica* consisted of pairs of back and front plates and overlapping hinged shoulder strips falling over the upper part of the arms. In 1964 parts of three armours, two almost complete, were found in a wooden box at Corbridge. A study of these has enabled Mr. Russell Robinson to reconstruct accurate models of the cuirass and its variants (*Bonner Jahrbucher*, 172 (1972), 24–35). Round his neck the legionary wore a scarf (*focale*) to prevent the metal plates from chafing his skin. The other two types of armour were forms of mail, one made of interlocking rings and the other of small metal scales, sewn in overlapping rows on to a jerkin (pl. IIIb). Fragments of both types have been found in the excavations of the barrack blocks in the Deanery Field, Chester (*Liverpool Annals*, xi, no. 2, pl. III). Men of the auxiliary units wore both chain and scale mail, as a close study of Trajan's Column shows, confirming the tombstone reliefs. Legionaries continued to wear the *lorica segmenta* well into the second century but it was gradually replaced by mail.

The lower part of the body was protected by a wide belt with a sporran-like attachment (*cingulum militare*). This was separate from the harness which held the sword and dagger in position. The belt and sporran were both heavily studded with metal and the latter consisted of leather strips which swung between the legs on the march, or was looped up to the belt as shown on Trajan's Column. The legs were free of armour and protection was sacrificed for mobility. Centurions, who were mounted on the march, wore decorated bronze greaves over their shins. In cold climates such as that of Britain, and on winter campaigns, tight-fitting leather trousers (*bracæ*) reaching below the knee were allowed. In the infantry, a most important piece of equipment is the boot. The legionaries had a heavy, thick-soled sandal (*caliga*). Examples found on forts show at least four thicknesses of leather in the sole which was heavily studded with hollow-headed hob-nails. The sandal was fastened to the foot by thongs tied at the ankle and it appears from some sculptures that a cloth or fur lining was occasionally permitted. The effect must have been one of flexibility, coolness, comfort and durability, more assets than many types of modern army boots possess.

An important item of defensive equipment was the shield (*scutum*). The legionary was distinguished by a rectangular shield curved to fit the body, in contrast with the oval variety used by the auxiliaries. It was made of leather or plywood bound at the edges with metal strips. The boss in the centre (*umbo*) was hollow and on the inside was fixed the handgrip. A leather strap was also fitted to the inside of the shield for the forearm and another to enable it to be slung from the left shoulder on the march. The outer surface of the shield was covered with leather with gilt or silvered bronze mounts representing Jupiter's thunderbolt.

Vegetius tells us that each cohort had differently coloured shields. Some highly-decorated shields were found at Dura-Europos on the Upper Euphrates but these may have been for parades.

Below all this equipment the soldier wore a woollen tunic reaching to his knees. Tombstones show the lower front of this garment arranged in a series of sweeping curves, as if reflecting that symbol of citizenship, the *toga*. Next to his skin, he had a linen under-garment, which was probably washed and changed regularly, since a high standard of personal hygiene was enforced. To keep out cold and wet, every soldier had a thick woollen cloak (*sagum*), probably brown in colour.

The legionary was an engineer and builder, as well as a soldier, and carried his tools with him. Josephus (*Wars of the Jews*, pt. iii, chap. 5), tells us that each soldier carried a saw, basket, pickaxe, a thong of leather, a chain, a sickle and three days' rations. On Trajan's Column some of these items can be seen attached to a staff or forked stick (to which was also tied the *pilum murale*) carried over the left shoulders of the legionaries as they march across the Danube, over the bridge of boats (pl. VIIb). A tool bag, very much like modern examples, is plainly discernible, also the wicker basket used for moving the earth from the ditch-digging to form the rampart. Each soldier has also a bronze mess-tin and kettle for cooking.

The pickaxe (*dolabra*) was slung from the belt, its sharp blade being housed in a special bronze sheath, a fragment of which can be seen in one of the museum cases. The only equipment not carried by the men was the leather tent (*papilio*) and the pair of millstones for grinding their food ; these cumbrous and heavy articles were borne by a mule shared by a tent party of eight men.

Officers' Dress.

The centurions and other officers wore distinctive uniforms. The body was protected by mail cuirass and shoulder plates and the sword was carried on the left-hand side. They also had a pleated leather kilt and boots of a more ornamental character than those of the soldiers.

Centurions carried a stout vine staff (*vitis*) (pl. Ic) as a symbol of their rank and did not hesitate to use it on the backs of the legionaries. High ranking officers wore an elaborate cloak (*paludamentum*), coloured white, red or purple according to status.

V

TERMS OF SERVICE AND PAY

THE conditions of legionary service and the pay varied considerably from time to time. When Augustus reorganized the Army on a completely professional basis, the legionary's service was fixed at 16 successive years, plus four years as a veteran with exemption from fatigues ; on discharge with a clean record, he received a grant of land in one of the chartered towns (*coloniæ*) especially founded for this purpose. In A.D. 6 these conditions were altered ; the period of service was lengthened to 20 years, the period as a veteran to five years and a grant of money made instead on discharge. The position was, however, very unsatisfactory as in many cases veterans were kept in the army long after they should have received their discharge. Tiberius did little to satisfy this grievance as he considered that the treasury could not afford a sudden series of mass donatives. The Flavian emperors eventually fixed the length of service at 25 years with discharges made every other year. The special corps of veterans formed by Augustus disappeared by the second century ; the old soldiers served normally in the legion but were exempt from fatigues.

Under Augustus, the legionary received payments of 300 *sesterces* three times a year but Domitian increased the yearly total to 1,200 *sesterces* and made the payments quarterly. In addition to this each legionary received a lump sum payment when a new emperor was enthroned, which helped to secure the loyalty of the army. It was the practice, however, for half the donative to be credited to the troops in the form of compulsory savings.

Originally when the army was based on a part-time citizen basis, the pay or *stipendium* was merely to cover expenses and the cost of food, clothing and equipment was deducted. This arrangement

continued into Imperial times. When the legions mutinied in
A.D. 14, Tacitus (*Annals*, i, 17, 6) tells us that one of their main
grievances was that they had to pay for their arms, clothing and
tents. The fact that food was not included may be because this
was accepted as a reasonable demand and the allowance deducted
so regularly that it was not noticed, whereas the other deductions
fell at different, unpredictable times. The statement which has
survived among the Egyptian papyri (*P. Gen. Lat.* i, quoted by
G. R. Watson, *The Roman Soldier*, Appendix A) appears to be not an
actual pay chit but a record made by those in charge of the bank of the
men's outstanding credits. This shows quite clearly the deduction
for food as about one-third of the total pay each time, whereas
clothing and equipment, also totalling about a third of the year's
pay, were deducted in different amounts at each pay day. These
items presumably varied according to the soldier's requirements
and his renewal of these necessary items.

In enemy territory the army lived off the land and deductions may
then have been quite small. Smaller items were deducted also for
the annual feast at Saturnalia, equivalent to our Christmas
festivities, and for the burial club. The latter money was handed
over to the standard bearers to ensure proper funeral rites, for at
all costs the spirit of the departed must be sent happily on its long
journey, lest it return and haunt those who neglected this solemn
duty.

Centurions were paid at a much higher rate and under Domitian
received as much as 5,000 *denarii* a year, nearly 17 times as much as a
legionary, and the *primi ordines* or centurions of the first cohort were
paid twice as much ; the *primus pilus bis* who was, in effect, the
C.O's aide, received 30,000 *denarii*, precisely a hundred times as
much as a private.

The pay of other ranks is a thorny problem. Those designated as
duplicarii received double the standard pay and *sesquiplicarii*, pay
and a half. It is far from clear precisely which particular officers
were so favoured. It seems strange but is, however, true, that a
large number of ranks carrying responsibility received no more pay
than a private. These included the *cornicines* and the *optiones
valetudinarii* and presumably ordinary *optiones*. Their rank, however, conveyed privileges, the chief one being exemption from
fatigues. Certain higher ranks of *principales* such as the *armorum
custodes*, *cornicularii* and *actuarii* were *duplicarii*, while some *librarii*
and *exacti* (tax collectors) were *sesquiplicarii*.

P. A. Brunt (*Papers Brit. School at Rome*, xviii, p. 71) has published
the following table in *denarii*, most of which is very tentative, the only
certain figures being the pay of a private under Augustus and Domitian:

Thirty

		Augustus	Domitian	Severus	Caracalla
Private ...	...	225	300	500	750
Highest class of					
principales ...	...	675	900	1,500	2,250
Centurions ...	...	3,750	5,000	$8,333\frac{1}{3}$	12,500
Primi ordines ...	...	7,500	10,000	16,666	25,000
Primi pili ...	...	15,000	20,000	$33,333\frac{1}{3}$	50,000

It is difficult to interpret these amounts in modern terms. It has been suggested (R. W. Moore, *The Roman Commonwealth*, p. 111) that the soldier's pay was equivalent to sixpence a day. On the other hand, there is evidence that he could live reasonably well on two-thirds of his pay. Taking corn as a standard, since this was his basic food, 60 *modii* would keep him for a year and a *modius* usually cost one *denarius*. Thus he had sufficient corn per week for just over a day's pay or, under Domitian, a fifth of his pay would have gone in corn.

Little is known of the arrangements for leave but it is clear that they existed. One reason for the failure of the ill-fated campaign of Pætus in Armenia during the reign of Nero was that so many soldiers had been given leave that the remainder were easily over-run by the vigilant enemy.

VI

DECORATIONS

UNDER the Empire the award of decorations for bravery and distinguished service became standardized according to ranks as in the British Army. Only one award, the *corona civica*, appears to have been given like a V.C., irrespective of rank. This decoration was awarded for saving the life of a fellow soldier, but appears to lapse after Claudius. It was given, according to Tacitus (*Annals*, xii, 31, 7), to the son of the governor Ostorius Scapula during his service in Britain. Other kinds of crowns were originally given for specific services, e.g., the *corona muralis*, awarded to the first centurion to lead the attack over the wall of a besieged town.

Other decorations were pairs of collars (*torques*), armlets (*armillæ*) and sets of circular discs (*phaleræ*), of which nine were usually awarded and worn over the cuirass on a leather harness (pl. Ic). These awards were available to centurions and other ranks. Tribunes and *legati* could win the *hasta pura* and the *vexillum*, which were model silver spear heads and standards like the modern baton, and the more senior the *legatus*, the more of these decorations could be worn. A *legatus consularis* regularly received four of each, and a *tribunus laticlavius* two of each. These decorations were worn or carried only on ceremonial parades but (like helmet plumes) these are quite often shown on sepulchral representations of the deceased.

VII

THE LEGIONARY FORTRESS

THE legion occupied either a marching camp or a permanent fortress according to circumstances. The former was set up during a campaign when the troops carried their leather tents with them. They were usually occupied for only a short time and the whole army group was encamped together, auxiliaries with legionaries. Although the tents were packed closely together, some of the camps were large in area; for example Raedykes in Scotland is about 114 acres in extent.

The only remains of this type of camp likely to have survived are the defences. These consisted of a small turf rampart, five or six feet high, behind a ditch. The gates were simple openings protected by a *clavicula* or curved extension of the rampart, or a *titulum* (formerly but erroneously known as *tutulus, Arch. Camb.* cxviii (1969), 133–134) or short ditch in front of the gate. The function of these was to force attackers to approach the gate in an oblique line with their right, and unprotected, sides exposed to the defenders' missiles. These types of camp are described in the pages of Polybius and Hyginus and have in the past been too readily confused with the more permanent forts.

If it was necessary to occupy hostile territory during the winter or if the campaign was successful, the newly conquered area was occupied by means of forts placed at strategic river crossings and joined together by a carefully planned road system. The forts were usually so spaced that they were no further apart than a day's march. These forts were built for single units or sometimes only detachments. The defences were stronger than those of the marching camp, and included gates and towers: all the buildings were of timber except the bath house which was provided from the early Flavian period onward, and was placed outside the defences.

Claudio-Neronian forts in Britain show considerable variety in layout, but from the Flavian period fort plans become much more uniform, even stereotyped. The general layout was the same. Whereever possible level ground was selected and the fort laid out in the form of a rectangle with rounded corners. The centre of the fort was occupied by the headquarters building or *principia*. The main road, the *via principalis*, crossed the fort in front of this building and was joined by another, the *via prætoria*, at its centre, forming a T-junction. These two roads led to three of the gates and a fourth gave access to the rear of the fort.

The rampart was built of material from the ditches strengthened at back and front with carefully stacked turfs and occasionally revetted in timber. Vegetius (iii, 8) tells us that the turves were cut with special tools to precise measurements, in Roman feet one by one and a half, and a half thick. This operation is clearly shown in a scene on Trajan's Column (Cichorius, xx ; Richmond, fig. 5). There were towers at intervals along the rampart and at the corners a platform was constructed for mounting a large catapult (*ballistarium*). The buildings conformed very much to type but every fort produced its own variations due to the peculiarities of the unit and local needs. There were several different kinds of auxiliary regiments. both of infantry and cavalry and provision was made for stables, fodder stores, as well as for varying types of equipment. Every fort had its *principia*, *prætorium* (commandant's quarters), barrack blocks and *horrea* (granaries), and the larger ones had additional stores, workshops and a hospital.

Legionary fortresses, built and planned on the same lines, were much larger and more elaborate. The area was about 50 to 60 acres, roughly ten times as large as the average auxiliary fort. Apart from the Agricolan fortress at Inchtuthil, Perthshire (*De Vita Agricolæ*, ed. by R. N. Oglivie and I A. Richmond, 1967, fig. 9), very little is known about the timber phase of the fortresses in Britain and only one, at Hofheim on the Rhine, has been excavated elsewhere. At the beginning of the second century, under Trajan, all the timber forts were dismantled and replaced with stone structures, the turf ramparts receiving stone-faced walls. Only two legionary fortresses have been completely excavated: those of *Novæsium* (Neuss) on the Rhine (pl. VIc) and *Carnuntum* on the Danube. The former produced better results since the latter had been more intensely occupied and altered. Most of the buildings at Neuss have been identified and there is everything one might expect to find in a large military depot, from the large granaries with reserve stocks to the prison with its small cells by the main gate.

In auxiliary forts it is normal to find the bath house in the annexe outside the fort, presumably to facilitate drainage and avoid the obvious fire risk. In legionary fortresses, however, these very large and elaborate buildings are accommodated within the walls. The bath house at Chester was in the south-east part of the fortress and that at Caerleon has been found in a similar position. At both fortresses there were additional bath buildings outside the defences. The amphitheatre was too large a building to place conveniently inside the fortress. At Chester it has been found near the south-east corner of the fortress, and almost half of it has now been excavated. This building, initially timber built, had a large open arena with tiered seats supported by a heavily buttressed external wall, and was used primarily for celebrating official festivals and for tactical demonstrations. It could be turned into a sports stadium for the amusement of the troops.

Relatively little is known about the arrangement of the buildings in the Chester fortress, since it lies beneath the modern city. However, a number of rescue excavations over the past twenty years have provided information about the *principia, prætorium* (?), granaries, the internal bath building, workshops, and barracks in the *prætentura* and *retentura*, as well as the defences (fig.1). More is known about Caerleon, where there have been extensive spaces available for excavations. Of the internal arrangements at York very little is at present known.

THE DEFENCES.

Roman military defences were designed not only to prevent the enemy entering the camp by a sudden assault but also to be proof against siege tactics like those at Jotapata described above.

The most dangerous weapons against mural fortifications were the battering ram and the miners' sap or tunnel. The ram, used with steady persistence, would make a breach in a stone or brick wall while tunnels cut under angles or corners in the wall could be made to create a serious collapse. Against the walls of the Near Eastern cities (made commonly of sun-dried bricks) these tactics were very effective.

To counter this threat, the Roman military engineers used the rampart. As indicated above, a turf rampart was the normal defence of a marching camp ; the more permanent the fort, the greater the necessity to strengthen the rampart and this was done by raising its height and increasing its thickness. The rampart of the Flavian (i.e., *c.* A.D. 75) fortress at Chester is 20 feet wide at its base and was perhaps as much as 18 feet high to the patrol track. A barrier as solid as this, stiffened at back and front with laid turves built on a platform of logs carefully laid at right-angles to the direction of the rampart, would be very difficult to breach with a ram. To give greater protection and also to arrest deterioration, this rampart, like most of those at other forts, was provided early in the second century with a stone wall or skin on the outer surface. At Chester this was a retaining wall only four feet thick. The thickness of the rampart had another advantage in providing the defenders with a platform six to ten feet wide on which to operate. They were, as in the reconstruction at Lincoln (fig. 2), protected by a breastwork of withies, or if the rampart was fronted with masonry, a two-foot wall to the same height. Above this, at intervals of 10 to 12 feet along the wall, were the merlons rising to another two feet, which gave total protection to any soldier standing behind them.

Towers were placed at intervals along the wall. These not only gave protection to the watch on patrol during inclement weather, but provided the defenders with a raised platform from which missiles could be discharged to a greater range than from the rampart top. Several timber towers are shown on Trajan's Column (Cichorius, Taf. xii) and the foundations of similar ones in stone were found at Chester (C.A.J. 56 (1969), 1–21; *Annals*, xxii, p. 19, and xxiii, p. 10). The spacing seems to be at about 150 feet centres and their overall dimensions about 23 ft. by 15 ft. Other towers were built within the rounded corners of the defences.

The approach to the rampart was protected by a system of ditches ; these varied in number and character with the potential hostility of the enemy. Where the Romans felt uneasy, they tended to increase the number of ditches; sometimes, however, they used a system of Punic ditches like the examples found by Prof. Richmond at Newstead, associated with a thorn hedge (*Proc. Soc. Ant. Scot.*, lxxxiv, p. 12). This type of ditch had a vertical outer face, probably in Britain revetted in timber, and a gently sloping inner one. The approaching enemy could easily jump on to the inner slope and collect on the berm at the foot of the rampart. Here they would be vigorously assaulted by missiles hurled from the rampart top and forced to retreat. The return journey was more difficult since it was impossible to jump from the sloping side on to the top of the vertical one and each man had to climb the latter, seriously hampered by the thorn hedge, and in so doing present an admirable target to the defenders on the rampart top waiting with their missiles.

The normal ditch was V-shaped (*fossa fastigata*) with sides steep enough to make crossing difficult and wide enough at the top to prevent anyone jumping across. At the same time, they were not so deep as to present the enemy with dead ground in which he could crouch to recover his breath. The whole of the ditch was

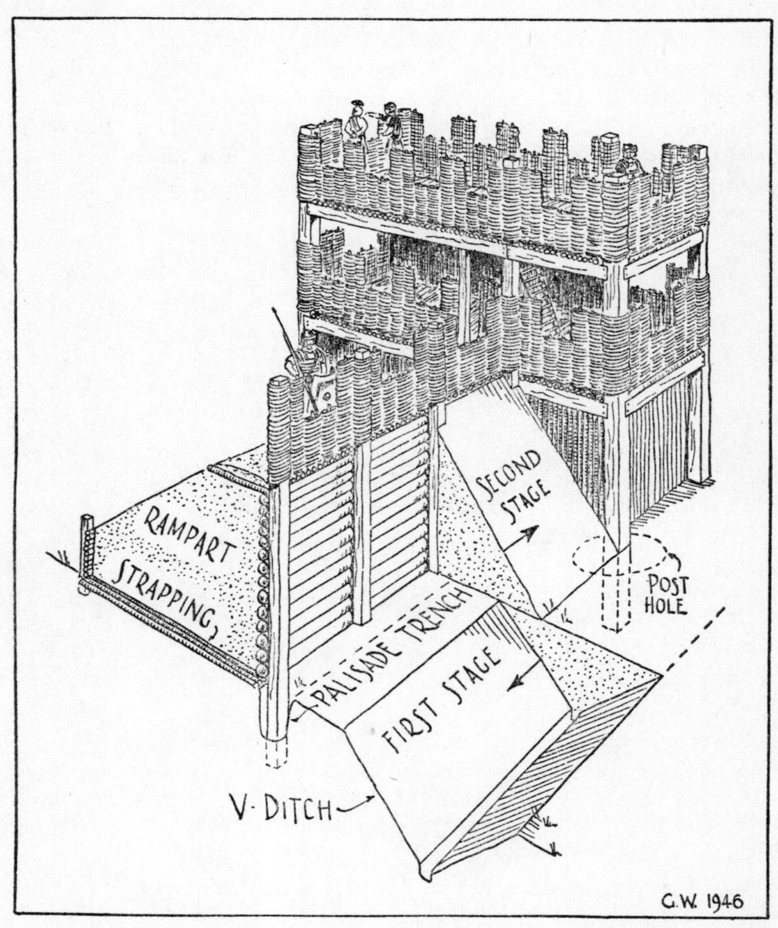

Fig. 2. *A reconstruction of the legionary defences at Lincoln.*

usually under observation from the rampart top. The ditches were kept cleaned out and a small channel, the width of a shovel, was made at the bottom for this purpose. There is evidence at Chester that the ditches may also have been drained. The ditch sides could be made less assailable by covering them with clay or a thorn hedge which would have the effect of modern barbed wire. This hedge, securely pegged to the ditch side, would not be visible to an attacking force and those in the front would probably jump straight into it with demoralising results. Chester, like Caerleon, had only one ditch, a fairly large one 23 ft. wide across the top, although this may be due to later recutting. An interesting feature is that on three sides of the fortress there is no berm ; the base of the original turf rampart which later became the front of the stone wall is also the beginning of the slope of the inner side of the ditch. This accounts for the great depth needed for the wall foundations.

The ditch was not the only form of defence beyond the rampart. The *titulum* or short ditch in front of a gate of marching camps has already been mentioned and a development of this was a system of pits (*lilia*). This uncommon device was probably used in special circumstances, an example in Britain being the Agricolan fort of Rough Castle (Macdonald, p. 235 and pl. XLIII). They are mentioned by Cæsar (*De Bell. Gall.*, vii, 73) and appear on Trajan's Column in front of a Dacian fort (Cichorius, Taf. xxv). This example may, however, merely demonstrate the use Decebalus made of the Roman engineers loaned by Domitian under treaty.

The scheme was to dig pits about 3 feet deep in rows, *quincunx* fashion, but allowing for an overlap. A stake with sharpened end uppermost was fixed in the centre of each pit, the top of which was concealed by a covering of leaves and brushwood. The enemy, rushing a vital point of the defences which the pits screened, would fall into them with unpleasant results and one can appreciate the ironic humour behind their name—lilies.

The four gates of the fortress were of solid construction but simple design. The actual doors were arranged in pairs with either a vaulted or open space between them. The opening was protected by towers, one on each side, and the patrol walk continued over it. In the first and second centuries there were none of the strong and cunning devices, copied and developed in the Middle Ages, which made castles so impregnable.

The only Roman gate at Chester of which any record has survived is the Eastgate, part of which was left embodied in the mediæval gate. Stukeley described what he saw in 1725, " I observed immediately two arches of Roman work still visible. It was a square of 20 ft. . . . in the same manner as at Lincoln (i.e., the Newport Arch, which is still standing) . . . on each side was a portal of a lesser arch." (*Itin. Cur.*, ii, p. 31.) His drawing, however, (*ibid.* pl. 65) shows merely his own suggestion of its original appearance. His original drawing, where he depicted the remains as he saw them, fortunately exists in the Bodleian Library (*MS. Top. gen. b.* 53(44)) and this clearly shows two main arches, only one of which had been used by the mediæval builders. It must have been a truly magnificent gate as the model suggests (pl. IVb). Unfortunately the whole gate was demolished in 1767 and Chester lost what would have been a great archæological treasure.

THE GENERAL LAYOUT OF THE FORTRESS.

All fortresses had the same basic layout. Where local conditions were favourable, the plan was rectangular. The central position was occupied by the *principia* or headquarters and the main street, the *via principalis*, passed across its front. The other main street, the *via prætoria*, met it at right angles in front of the *principia* so that the two streets formed a T-junction. The only other street of importance was the *via quintana* which was parallel to the *via principalis* but passed at the rear of the *principia* for the full width of the fortress. Access was gained to the other buildings by means of narrow lanes. It was tactically desirable to have ready access to the defences from all points of the fortress ; this was provided by the intervallum road (*via sagularis*) which ran the whole way round the perimeter of the fortress behind the rampart. This feature also helped to create a space and place the outermost buildings beyond the range of enemy missiles, some of which were of an incendiary character.

Ideally the fortress and front of the *principia* faced the enemy so that theoretically the wild barbarians could look down the *via prætoria* through the *principia* entrance across the great courtyard and beyond the basilican cross-hall towards the ornamental screen of the sanctuary where dwelled the gods on the side of the big battalions. Since the Chester fortress faced south, we must assume that the enemies to be overlooked and so overawed were those sturdy Welsh tribes which resisted the imperial advance so stoutly.

The fortress was divided into two unequal parts by the *via principalis*, the *prætentura* and the *retentura*. The more important buildings such as the commandant's quarters (*prætorium*) and hospital (*valetudinarium*) occupied central positions ; the barrack blocks, about 24 pairs of them, were placed at the two extremities except those of the five double centuries of the first cohort which were normally to be found in line with the *principia*.

The *principia* or headquarters block was the administrative and spiritual centre of the fortress. It was divided into three distinct parts. At the front was a large open courtyard surrounded on three sides by ranges of buildings and colonnaded pavements. The main ceremonies and drill practices were carried out on the large parade ground outside the fortress, but the presence in the courtyard of altars and *tribunalia* (saluting bases) shows that ceremonies and parades were also customary there. Another feature of the courtyard was a well to provide an emergency water supply should the fortress be invested ; it was also needed for the pack animals which brought in the stores. The latter were kept in the three ranges of buildings around the courtyard. In the opinion of some, each century had its own stores but it is more likely that materials were brought to the *principia* and stored in bulk. This is certainly the impression received from the fragmentary evidence from Lambæsis. The second part of the *principia* beyond the courtyard was the great cross-hall or basilica. This large hall with its two rows of massive columns flanked by aisles must have been very similar to the nave of a Norman cathedral, which was its architectural successor. The cross-hall at Chester was about 240 feet long, the total width was 80 feet, the span of the nave being 40 feet and each aisle 20 feet. It would have been possible to assemble the bulk of the Legion here providing the soldiers stood shoulder to shoulder, and the commander or a visiting dignitary could have spoken to them, read an order of the day or issued special instructions. These assemblies may have been associated with the legionary shrine which stood in the centre, its door built into the wall of the aisle. There must have been ceremonies at the opening of a campaign when the standards were brought from their resting places with much pomp and ritual.

Excavations in 1969 revealed part of this shrine, and also the range of rooms alongside it which opened in a similar way into the aisle of the cross-hall (*C.A.J.* 57 (1970–71) 3–26). At Chester the shrine (*sacellum*) contained a large rock-cut strong room for the pay chests, but such a strong room was not found at Caerleon (*Arch. Camb.*, 119 (1971) 19–21). In these rooms on either side of the shrine the administration of the legion was carried out, correspondence was received, answered and filed, accounts were kept, and the pay clerks worked out the many deductions from the soldiers' pay.

The whole building was of monumental proportions, dwarfing the barrack blocks and most of the other adjacent buildings. The decoration of the cross-hall at Chester was crude but effective and from surviving fragments, Professor Richmond has said

" . . . it is of special interest to see how the military stonemason or provincial carver, faced with the problem of providing architectural detail of an elaboration to which the military mind was unaccustomed, reduced the elements of a purely classical design to his own terms and produced a result which probably harmonised better with the general treatment of the building than a rigid adherence to Mediterranean practice would have done " (*C.A.J.*, 38 (1951), 35).

The *prætorium* or commandant's house was a building almost as large as the *principia* and was usually adjacent to it either along the *via principalis* or the *via quintana*. The building, which may also have been used as an officers' mess, was an elaborate courtyard house with heated rooms and a small bath suite, the only building inside the fortress containing these amenities. Its position at Chester is not certain although recent excavations (*C.A.J.*, 55 (1968), 1; 57 (1970–71), 3–26) suggest that it may have been north of the *principia*. The tribunes' houses were smaller versions of the *prætorium*.

At Chester a large internal bath house measuring 263 ft. east-west by 274 ft. north-south has been identified in the southern part of the fortress immediately east of the *via prætoria* (Bridge Street). An inscription from a large covered exercise hall at its northern end indicates that it dates from the earliest period, i.e. when the rest of the fortress was in timber. Much of the plan was recovered during building work on the site in 1964, under far from ideal circumstances which did not permit full examination of this remarkable building.

The baths were housed in a large building with specialised functions (pl. Va). The Romans, brought up in the traditions of an urban Mediterranean culture, regarded a bath as a natural part of the daily routine of civilized men. Their idea was, however far removed from the solitary soak of modern convention. The bath was shared with one's colleagues or fellow-citizens and accompanied by exercise, massage and indoor games. The baths were, in fact, a social club where one normally spent a happy hour or so, stripping off the cares of life as well as its toil and sweat. This was naturally encouraged by the army authorities, since hygiene was an important factor in the health of the soldiers. Ample bath houses were provided for all forts, great and small. They were usually placed in the annexe outside the fort for two good reasons. In the first place the furnace presented a serious fire risk and it was better for the building to be kept well away from the rest of the camp which may, in the first century, have been constructed of timber. Secondly other units on the move spending the night under the shelter of the fort pitched their tents in the annexe and could make use of the bath house independently of the usual garrison.

The method of bathing was that of the Turkish bath which is, of course, a descendant of the Roman principle surviving through Byzantine times. There were several interconnecting rooms kept at different temperatures and the main idea was to work up a perspiration, if necessary, by exercise in the hot room where the atmosphere was permeated with steam. The bather could then be sluiced down with hot or warm water, retire to the cooler rooms and receive massage which included the rubbing of oils into the body. A more invigorating method was to go straight from the hot room into a cold plunge bath. The rooms were so arranged that bathers could pass easily from one to the other. The plunge baths were usually small and it seems to have been more usual for water to have been supplied from basins or cauldrons. At convenient pauses in the routine, the bathers would lounge on mats and gossip or gamble.

As one can imagine from this short description, the bath houses were large and complex structures, carefully planned, soundly built and thoroughly insulated to retain the heat, with furnaces, hypocausts and hot air ducts and ample drainage and water supply.

The *valetudinarium* or hospital was an essential building in a large military depot. The example at Neuss was a long courtyard type of building with small cubicles opening inward. At the entrance was a large reception hall and at the end a small operating theatre with running water and arrangements for heating to raise the temperature and sterilize the instruments.

The *horrea* or granaries were buildings of characteristic design and construction (pl. Vb). It was vital that the basic food supplies should be given maximum protection to ensure the smallest possible loss. There were several dangers: the worst was fire. After the beginning of the second century, the granaries were solidly built of stone with tile or slate roofs. The latter was given a large overhang, so that the water from the eaves-drip was carried well clear of the building and this also afforded greater shade from the hot sun (pl. Vc). This explains the presence of piers at regular intervals along the side of the granary; they carried the roof timbers out beyond the walls as well as acting as buttresses. The floors of granaries were raised above ground level on sleeper walls to keep the grain dry. A system of ventilators in the walls below floor level ensured the free circulation of air. The floors were composed of flagging and special precautions were taken against rats and mice. The three granaries located at Chester (*C.A.J.*, 46, 33–60) were grouped together on the side of the fortress nearest the harbour; those at Inchtuthil were interspersed with the barracks. The best preserved granaries in Britain are probably those at Corbridge, a military depot behind the Wall, near Hexham (*A.A.*, 4th s., xxviii).

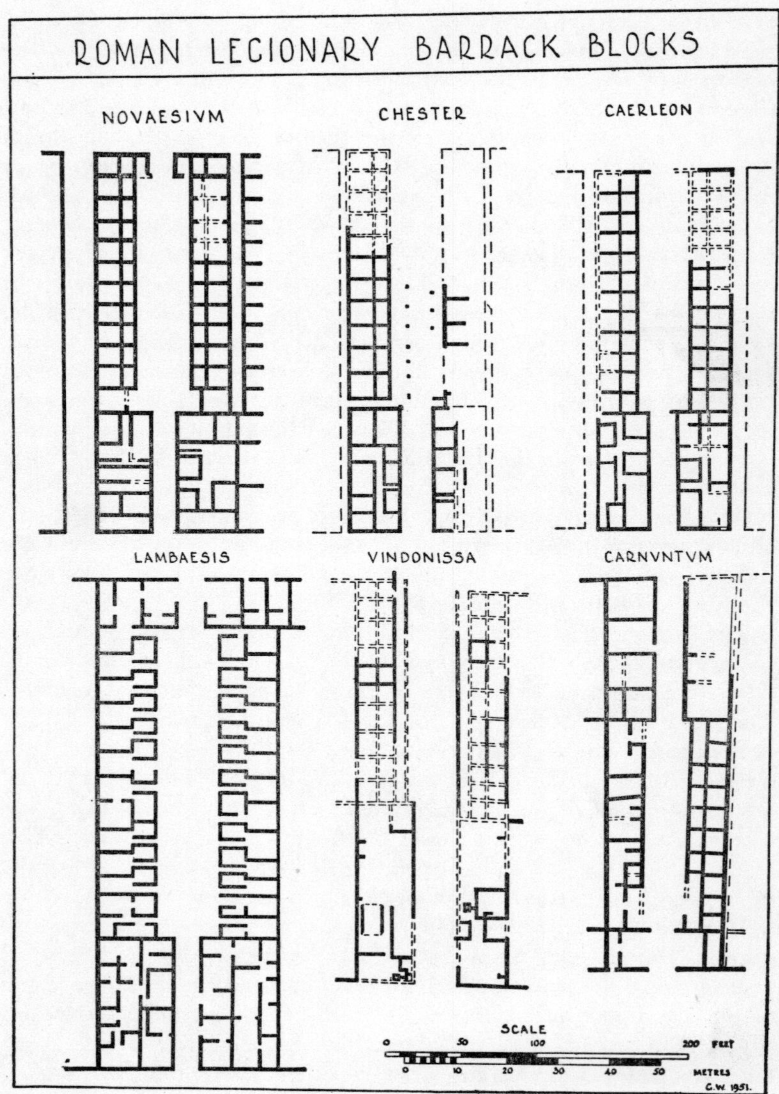

Fig. 3. *Comparative plans of barrack blocks.*

Several attempts have been made to calculate the capacities of granaries relative to the garrison (in particular Haverfield and Collingwood on " The Provisioning of Roman Forts " in *C.W.*, 2nd s., xx, and Richmond in *Proc. Soc. Ant. Scot.*, lxxiii, 129) but they are made difficult by the uncertainty as to whether the grain was stored in bulk or in barrels and also if other kinds of food such as meat were housed there as well.

Barrack blocks were arranged in pairs forming a complete *striga* accommodating two centuries of 80 men each (pl. Vd). This standardised plan, which seems to have been common throughout the Empire (fig. 3), developed from the way the leather tents were pitched in the marching camps (see " Tents of the Roman Army," by J. McIntyre and I. A. Richmond in *C.W.*, xxxiv, p. 62). Each section of eight men shared a tent and a mule ; the men slept in the tent and a space was left in front of it for the animal and baggage. In permanent quarters, each section shared two rooms, the inner one at Chester measuring about 15 ft by 13 ft. for sleeping, and the outer, about 9 ft. by 13 ft., for their equipment. Beyond this, running the full length of the block, was a verandah. Each sleeping room had a hearth, presumably for warmth and possibly also for cooking. At the end of each long block were the centurions' quarters with elaborate and non-standard internal partitioning. These quarters had refinements not to be found in the men's blocks. In the Deanery Field at Chester fragments of wall plaster were recovered from which it has been possible to reconstruct the original floral pattern. A drain was connected with one of the rooms indicating the presence of a latrine or washplace.

The floors of the barrack block are usually found to be of clay but they probably had wood planks or stone flags. There are no indications of any couching arrangements and it is probable that the men were supplied with straw mattresses which have left no trace. The other kinds of buildings to be found in a legionary fortress are stables, workshops, smithies, storehouses, cookhouses and ovens, and by the main gate a small prison.

The Extra-Mural Buildings.

It is usual to find a number of buildings outside the fortress. These may be official or belong to the civil settlement. There is one structure of the former category which was almost always built outside, the amphitheatre.

The amphitheatre was a large open arena, oval in plan, with a massive, heavily buttressed outer wall which supported tiers of seats (pl. IVc). The structure was designed to accommodate the full legionary complement of about 6,000 men. Although its purpose may have been primarily religious, for here were celebrated the festivals in the military calendar, such as the Emperor's birthday and those of his family, the birthday of the legion and many others which involved large-scale parades, it was useful also for training and tactical demonstrations. The amphitheatre has become best known for its association with gladiators and wild beast shows. While these had their place, no doubt, on a small scale in Britain, they were the " fun and games " after the serious and solemn festivals had finished. The amphitheatre at Chester lies outside the south-east corner of the fortress: almost half of the building has now been exposed and may be visited. This is the largest amphitheatre so far found in Britain, measuring 334 ft. by 278 ft. (report forthcoming; see also Ancient Monuments guide leaflet by F. H. Thompson). In the centre was found an unexplained timber platform *c.* 7.6 x 2.7 m. The excavations also produced a small altar to the goddess of Fate (Nemesis) put up by a centurion after a dream. The amphitheatre at Caerleon, excavated in 1926–7, is completely exposed (*Archæologia* 78, 111).

Other buildings outside the fortress consisted of storehouses by the harbour, the private houses of those officers who could afford them, and temples built and maintained by private benefactors. There was also a sizeable parade ground where large-scale reviews and ceremonies could have been held, judging by the altars which are sometimes found nearby (e.g., Maryport, *A.A.*, n.s., vii (1871), p. 184).

THE CIVIL SETTLEMENT

One of the features of a Roman camp of any size was the *canabæ* or huts of the civilian squatters who settled down outside the defences. There were considerable commercial advantages in being near a body of troops with regular pay. The harsh discipline of the Roman army made out-of-camp attractions all the more alluring. Drink, food and the usual kind of entertainments gave their promoters rich dividends. It is little wonder that the crude shanty-town which first sprang up gradually gave place to buildings of a more permanent and substantial character, often reflecting the wealth of the occupants. These settlements sometimes became administrative centres and were invested with the dignity of civic status, like York, which became a *colonia*. In times of peace, there were regular fairs to which pedlars, traders and entertainers would be attracted and it is interesting to reflect that some of the large European cities of today have sprung from such lowly origins.

Little is known of the civil settlement at Chester. It has always

Forty-four

been thought to have been outside the east gate. There has certainly
been a considerable quantity of pottery found in this area but only
slight evidence of any buildings. On the other hand, there is a large
settlement known to exist about two miles south of Chester at
Heronbridge, the purpose of which is not at present understood.
It would have been unusual, but not impossible, for this to have been
the civil settlement which Professor E. Birley considers may have
had municipal status (*C.A.J.*, xxxvi, p. 173). Excavations have revealed typical domestic strip buildings with evidence of metal
working and perhaps a dock (*C.A.J.*, xxx; xxxix, p. 3; xli, p. 15.

Cemeteries

Under the Twelve Tables, the Romans were not permitted to
bury their dead inside towns or military fortresses. On the whole
they kept strictly to this law except for infant burials and murders
or accidents. If, therefore, one discovers burials other than these
casual deposits inside a fortress, as in the case of the three cremations
found in the north-east corner at Chester, it is certain that they
belong to a period preceding the establishment of the fortress. It was
customary to line the roads entering the town with cemeteries like
the famous Appian Way in Rome. Doubtless the best and most
expensive plots were those nearest the road. Many of the plots
were purchased for the family and a number of burials anticipated.

The monuments differed according to the method of disposal.
Both cremation and inhumation were practised in Roman times ;
the former was universal in the first century but slowly gave place
to the latter until that, in turn, was more popular by the late second
century. Cremation burials had the advantage of occupying
less space and a family tomb could have been constructed to take
a number of burials. After the body was burnt on a pyre, a token
handful of ashes was placed in a vessel of glass or pottery or
occasionally in a lead canister and this in turn put into the tomb
which was opened for the purpose. This practice gave rise to the
development of elaborate monuments like little houses or temples
and a number of examples of this kind of tomb are to be found in
the large Chester collection. In the cases of poorer people the
vessels were merely buried in the ground with probably their necks
showing and it may be that the interesting type of face mask jar
was used for this purpose. Inhumations were placed in coffins of
wood or lead and buried below the ground, usually without any
further protection, but at Chester the soldiers favoured tile-lined
and roofed graves. The memorial in these cases was a simple
upright slab with an inscription and possibly a relief of the deceased.

One practice was common to both types of disposal—the placing of the deceased's personal objects and some food in the grave. The food and drink was normally a mere token and left in small vessels. The mourners poured sweet smelling perfumes and oils from little glass bottles into the grave and left them there. It is thought that these may also have contained the tears of the mourners. The Chester burials in the Infirmary Field area revealed several interesting features. All objects had been deliberately broken before being placed in the grave. In some cases, a hole had been made in the base of a bowl and the tiny fragments which fitted into it were found in the grave. In another instance a hand mirror had been broken and the pieces carefully placed in a vessel much too small to have contained the intact object.

The Chester cemeteries are very extensive and line the roads to the east and south. There are also a number of groups of burials on the north and west sides of the fortress. It is probable that they belong to different dates ; the large cemetery, for example, in the Handbridge area has produced vessels of the third century. The most important burials from the historical aspect are those from the Deanery Field. These cremations inside the fortress must belong to a period before the latter existed and are at present the only indication we have of an earlier phase, probably consisting of a small auxiliary fort built about A.D. 58, associated with the campaigns of Quintus Veranius and Suetonius Paullinus in North Wales.

DRAINAGE AND WATER SUPPLY.

These were very important features, closely associated with the health of the legionaries, and the Roman military engineers always went to considerable lengths to see that both were adequate. It was their main purpose to see that running water was supplied to the more important buildings and used to flush the latrines. At Chester the supply was the springs in the sand at Boughton near Cherry Grove and the water was led by gravity into the fortress. At the source was a shrine graced by a fine altar, now at Eaton Hall, dedicated to the nymphs of the fountains. A lead supply pipe, bearing an inscription—the only one so far found in Britain—was recovered in 1899 from the north side of Eastgate Street.

Drainage was not a difficult problem since the sewers could discharge by gravity into the river. In addition to the normal water supply, all the streets were lined with drains which removed the rain water discharged into the streets direct from the roofs. This practice accounts for the necessity for colonnaded walks along the sides of buildings. A large rock cut drain, probably of

Roman origin, is known to exist in Pepper Street running towards White Friars. This is of considerable depth and may have been to keep the ditch dry, making it easier to maintain.

FOR FURTHER READING

Sources.

A. Primary—Much information concerning the Roman Army at the different phases of its history can be obtained from the Roman historians. Those who worked from first-hand experience like Cæsar (*Gallic Wars*, etc.), Josephus (*Wars of the Jews*), and Arrian (*Tactics*) are the best. There are also Polybius (*History of the Romans*), Tacitus (*Annals, Histories* and *Agricola*), Ammianus Marcellinus, and Frontius (*Stratagems*).

There are two works specifically on military matters. *Instituta Rei Militaris*, a late compilation by Vegetius, is indispensable (an English translation was published by J. Clarke in 1767—an abridged version appeared in *Roots of Strategy* edited by Major T. R. Phillips, 1943). An anonymous work, *De Munitionibus Castrorum*, gives much useful information on military defences and marching camps; the best edition of the latter is that of von Domaszewski, Leipzig, 1887.

The finest pictorial account is Trajan's Column, which is fully illustrated and described by Cichorius (*Die Reliefs der Traianssäule*, Berlin, 1896–1900); a better text but poorer illustrations is provided by Lehmann-Hartleben (*Die Traianssäule*. Berlin and Leipzig, 1926). The best account in English, with a penetrating analysis of army methods and equipment, has been written by Professor I. A. Richmond (Trajan's Army on Trajan's Column—*Papers of the British School at Rome*, xiii).

Many details of equipment are given on military tombstones, especially those found on the Rhine. Most of them have been illustrated in the volumes of *Germania Romana*. Fragments of actual weapons and equipment have been found in excavations. The finest British publication is undoubtedly J. Curle *A Roman Frontier Post and its People: The Roman Fort of Newstead*. Elsewhere are the extensive German and Austrian Limes excavations, published in the Commissions' Reports, and since 1959, in the *Limesforschungen*. Another interesting excavation report for remarkable finds of army equipment is that of the Yale University Expedition Report of Dura-Europos.

B. Secondary

General:

G. L. Cheesman, *The Auxilia of the Roman Imperial Army*, 1914.

H. M. D. Parker, *The Roman Legions*, Reprinted 1958.

P. Couissin, *Les Armes romaines*, 1926.

J. Kromayer and G. Veith, *Heerwesen und Kriegführung der Griechen und Römer*, Munich, 1928.

A. von Domaszewski, *Die Rangordnung des römischen Heeres*, 2nd ed. by Dr. Brian Dobson, 1967.

G. R. Watson, *The Roman Soldier*, 1969.

Graham Webster, *The Roman Imperial Army*, 1968, with a full bibliography.

See also the important articles in Pauly-Wissowa, *Realencyclopädie*, Ritterling on *Legio* and Liebenam on *Exercitus* and in Daremberg-Saglio *Dictionnaire des Antiquités grecques et romaines*, 1874—, R. Cagnat on *Castra*, *Exercitus* and *Legio*. For the Army in the late Empire:— A. H. M. Jones, *The Later Roman Empire 284–602*, 1964, ii, chapter XVII

For the Army in Britain and its Frontiers:

 V. E. Nash-Williams, *The Roman Frontier in Wales*, 2nd ed., edited by Michael G. Jarrett, 1969.

 J. C. Bruce, *Handbook to the Roman Wall*, 12th ed., by I. A. Richmond, 1965.

 E. Birley, *Research on Hadrian's Wall*, 1961; and *Roman Britain and the Roman Army*, 1953, a valuable collection of papers.

 G. Macdonald, *The Roman Wall in Scotland*, 2nd ed., 1934.

 Anne S. Robertson, *The Antonine Wall*, 1968, a handbook published by the Glasgow Archaeological Society.

 P. Salway, *The Frontier People of Roman Britain*, 1965.

 Donald R. Dudley and Graham Webster, *The Roman Conquest of Britain*, 1965.

 Ordnance Survey, *Map of Hadrian's Wall*, 1964, (2 ins. to the mile) and *The Antonine Wall* ($2\frac{1}{2}$ inch), 1968.

For important papers on military sites in Britain see contributions in *Journal of Roman Studies, Britannia, Epigraphische Studien, Arch. Cambrensis, Arch. Aeliana*, etc.

On inscriptions and papyri:—

 R. G. Collingwood and R. P. Wright, *The Roman Inscriptions of Britain*, I. 1965.

 H. I. Bell, V. Martin, E. G. Turner and D. van Berchem, *The Abinnaeus Archive*, 1962.

 R. O. Fink—*Roman Military Records on Papyrus*, 1971.

For the Flavian campaigns B. W. Henderson's *Civil War and Rebellion in the Roman Empire*, 1908.

On weapons and equipment there are L. Lindenschmit, *Tracht und Bewaffnung des römischen Heeres während der Kaiserzeit*, 1882; J. Alfs, "*Der bewegliche Metallpanzer im römischen Heer*" in *Zeitschrift für*

historische Waffen-und Kostumkunde, Heft 3/4 (1941); an attractively
illustrated book by A. Forestier, *The Roman Soldier*, 1928; and
E. W. Marsden, *Greek and Roman Artillery—Historical Development*
(1969); *Technical Treatises* (1971).

On the Navy:
    Chester G. Starr, *The Roman Imperial Navy*, Cornell, 2nd edition,
       1960.

On supplies:
    Van Berchem, *L'Annone militaire dans l'Empire romain au III ème*
       Siècle.

On conscription and recruitment:
    G. Forni, *Il Reclutamento delle Legioni da Augusto a Diocleziano*, 1953.
    E. Birley, *Noricum, Britain and the Roman Army*, in *Beiträge zur*
       älteren europäischen Kulturgeschichte, Bd. I—*Festschrift für Rudolf*
       Egger, Klagenfurt, 1952.

On medical services:
    R. W. Davies, 'The Medici of the Roman Armed Forces', *Epig.*
       Studien, 3 (1969), 83–99.
    British Museum Guide to Greek and Roman Life, chap xviii.

An important article on religion in the Roman Army is by Prof. I. A.
Richmond, "Roman Legionaries at Corbridge, their supply base,
temples and religious cults" in *A.A.*[4], xxi (1943), p. 127, which is
based on the "Feriale Duranum" by Messrs. Fink, Huey and Snyder
in *Yale Classical Studies*, vii (1939).

On the Diploma:
    D. Atkinson, *The Wroxeter Excavations 1923–27*, reprinted 1969,
       chap. xv; *Corpus Inscriptionum Latinarum*, xvi, Berlin 1936, deals
       with *diplomata* and is indispensable to a study of the dispo-
       sitions of the auxilia.

On Legionary Fortresses:
       In Britain—

Caerleon   George C. Boon, *Isca*, published by the National
                 Museum of Wales, 1972, includes a full bibliography.
                 George C. Boon and Colin Williams, *Plan of Caerleon*
                 up to Dec. 1966, National Museum of Wales, 1967, with
                 useful comparative plans and bibliography.
                 Donald Moore, *Caerlon, Fortress of the Legion*, 1970, a
                 popular account.

Chester   F. H. Thompson, *Deva, Roman Chester* (1959).
                 F. H. Thompson, *Roman Cheshire* (1965).

Inchtuthil   I. A. Richmond, 'The Agricolan legionary fortress at
                 Inchtuthil', *Limes Studien, Vorträge des 3. Inter-*
                 nationalen Limes-Kongresses in Rheinfelden 1957, 1959,

        pp. 152–55, and annual reports in *J.R.S.*

York   R.C.H.M., *Eburacum: Roman York*, 1962.

Lincoln   I. A. Richmond, *Arch. J.*, 103 (1967), 26–29.

        F. H. Thompson, *J.R.S.* 46 (1956), 22–36.

        Elsewhere—

Aquincum   V. Kuzsinszky, *Aquincum, Ausgrabungen und Funde*, 1934.

        J. Szilágyi, *Aquincum*, 1956.

Carnuntum   von Groller, excavation reports in *Der römische Limes in Österreich*, Heft I to X and XII.

        E. Swoboda, *Carnuntum: Römische Forschungen in Niederösterreich*, Band I, 1964, for the most up-to-date summary.

Lambaesis   R. Cagnat, *Les Deux Camps*, and a summary in *L'Armée romaine d'Afrique*.

Lauriacum   W. A. Jenny and H. Vetters, *Forschungen in Lauriacum*, Band I, 1953.

Mainz   D. Baatz, *Moguntiacum, Limesforschungen*, 4 (1962).

Nijmegen   J. E. Bogaers, 'Romeins Nijmegen', *Numaga*, 12 (1965) pp. 10ff. P. Stuart, *Gewoon aardewerk uit de romeinse legerplaats en de bijbehorende grafvelden te Nijmegen*, 1963, with a full bibliography. H. Brunsting, *400 Jaar romeinse bezetting van Nijmegen*, 1969, a useful and well illustrated booklet.

Novaesium   H. Lehner, 'Novaesium', *Bonner Jahrbucher*, 111–12

(Neuss)   (1904), excavation report.

        H. von Petrikovits, *Novaesium, Das römische Neuss*, 1957, and 'Die Ausgrabungen in Neuss', *Bonner Jahrbucher*, 161 (1961) 449–85.

Regensburg   A. Stroh, 'Untersuchung an der Sudostecke des Lagers der Legio III in Regensburg', *Germania*, 36 (1958), 78–79.

Vetera   Excavations in *Bonner Jahrbucher*, 124, 126, 139, and 159.

(Xanten)   H. Lehner, *Das Römerlager Vetera bei Xanten*, 1936, a short guide.

        H. Lorenz, *Untersuchungen zum Praetorium*, 1936.

Vindonissa   R. Laur-Belart, *Vindonissa: Lager und Vicus; Römisch-Germanische Forschungen*, 10, 1935, and interim and specialist reports in *Gesellschaft pro Vindonissa*.